THE HISTORY OF APARTHEID

By the same author

The Asiatic Danger in the Colonies
General Hertzog
Some South African Politicians
White Man's Africa
Today's News Today
City Built on Gold

THE HISTORY
OF APARTHEID

The Story of the Colour War
in South Africa

by

L. E. NEAME

Sometime Editor of the
Rand Daily Mail (Johannesburg)
the *Cape Argus* (Cape Town)

LONDON HOUSE & MAXWELL
NEW YORK

FIRST PUBLISHED IN THE UNITED STATES
OF AMERICA 1963 BY
LONDON HOUSE & MAXWELL
A DIVISION OF THE BRITISH BOOK CENTRE, INC.
122 EAST 55TH STREET, NEW YORK 22, NEW YORK
© L. E. NEAME 1962

Printed in the United States of America

CONTENTS

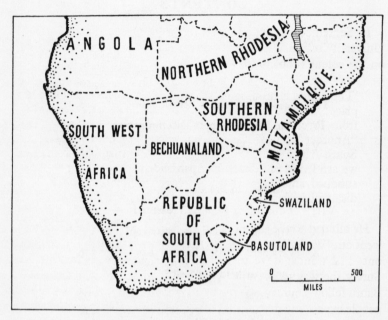

SOUTH AFRICA AFTER MAY 31, 1961.

PREFACE

In September, 1959, an ex-senior professor on the staff of the University of the Witwatersrand wrote a letter to the newspapers on the colour problem in South Africa. He said:

> 'The Union is heading for disaster. This is almost a commonplace: we have heard it from our friends abroad, we hear it from lovers of South Africa at home: we smile and say "Another Jeremiah" and turn to something more pleasant . . . South Africa is a good place for a White man to live in. But we are living in a fool's paradise. We close our ears to those subdued rumblings that precede a volcano's eruption or a disastrous earthquake.'

He alluded to the brutal flogging of Natives on some farms and went on: 'We indignantly deny that we have slavery in the country but . . . I wonder if we are really as innocent as we pretend to be. Surely the way to prevent bloodshed is to accord at once to our Bantu fellow-countrymen the basic human rights which we White people expect and demand as part of our human heritage. For there is no colour bar in God's justice.'

Two years earlier the National Executive of the South African Institute of Race Relations, an authorative study group, had felt compelled to issue a special appeal to all South African citizens. They said that repressive legislation and the undermining of all voluntary association with Africans had resulted in a tide of resentment which if continued 'will be tragic for all in our country' for the racial groups might become 'sealed off into entirely separate and hostile camps.' 'It is,' they added, 'with a heavy sense of responsibility and a heart-felt concern for the future of the country that we issue this grave statement. We call on our fellow South Africans, particularly on the Europeans who exercise sole political control, to take heed before it is too late.'

The small group of 'intellectuals' who study the colour question

7

utter similar warnings to a White population most of whom are too engrossed in business or sport to pay serious attention to those they regard as 'alarmists', or even worse, 'liberals'.

It is significant however that the Union Government, after sending two army officers to study the situation in war-torn Algeria, has increased its military forces and formed special units armed with the weapons most suitable for suppressing riots or revolts. It could—and doubtless would—put down any rising with a heavy hand. But it would be at the cost of fomenting the hatred which a great number of Blacks now feel for the Afrikaners, and probably extending it to all Whites.

The colour question in the Union is becoming a very dangerous issue because there seems to be no way in which it can be resolved by agreement, or even made to assume a more amenable shape.

On both sides the spirit of no compromise is hardening. The Whites are more than ever convinced that their supremacy in their homeland is seriously threatened, and they are determined to fight to the bitter end rather than be submerged in the Black ocean surrounding them. The Blacks, inspired by the upsurge of African nationalism that is sweeping across the continent, are demanding the repeal of what they regard as oppressive laws, and also the right to have some say in the government of the country in which they do most of the unskilled and semi-skilled work. They are encouraged in their claims by the success of their fellows in other parts of Africa in getting rid of all discriminatory laws and obtaining a share in the administration.

Thus in the Union the irresistible force of Black nationalism is rapidly moving towards the immovable body of White domination. What will the outcome be?

This book explains how the present crisis has been reached. It records the stages by which the practice of discriminating on the ground of colour of the skin has grown and been sanctioned by law. It sets out the arguments by which the colour bar is justified by one side and denounced by the other. It is an objective survey of the threatening situation in South Africa and the different measures by which it is hoped to avert a grave upheaval in the near future.

L. E. NEAME

Johannesburg, 1961

CHAPTER I

The Racial Background

The all-important problem in South Africa today is the future co-existence of Whites and Non-Whites.

For a hundred years the basic issue appeared to be that of race—the rivalry between Dutch and English. Now it is seen to be that of colour—the growing conflict between Europeans and Non-Europeans.

In other parts of the world the question of discrimination on the ground of the colour of the skin is being gradually, and in the main peacefully, resolved. There is a re-partitioning of the surface of the globe. Everywhere the Non-Whites insist that what they call 'colonialism' or 'imperialism' can no longer be tolerated. They hold that every race is entitled to govern the land in which it lives, or at least to share in its administration.

The majority of nations accept the new dispensation. The necessary political changes are being effected without serious upheavals. The White guardians who long guided and governed Non-White peoples are retiring with more or less grace leaving the future administration of the estate to their wards.

The Republic of South Africa refuses to fall into line. Its White rulers are not prepared to share authority with Non-Whites. They insist upon the political, social, industrial and residential separation of Europeans and Non-Europeans.

To distant observers the problem of colour in South Africa seems to differ very little from that in other lands in which a White minority co-exists with a Non-White majority. To them there appears to be no reason why the situation should not be handled as readily as it has been elsewhere. The less-developed majority have only to be given a share in the administration, which will be gradually increased as they advance in civilization, until

9

ultimately they attain full partnership on a basis of equal rights.

But there is a fundamental difference between South Africa and the territories in which Non-White majorities have been, or are being, groomed for eventual self-government. Lord Balfour realized this many years ago when he said: 'In South Africa a White nation has established itself in a Black continent, and that is something that has never before presented itself in the history of mankind.'

The operative word is 'nation'. It is the presence of a manifest White nation at the foot of the Dark Continent that has created a problem that has no counterpart elsewhere in the world.

In South Africa there is entrenched a White people three million strong. They form a nation numerically comparable with those in Eire and Denmark and Norway whose title to self-rule is not denied on the ground of inadequacy of numbers.

The European adventurers who went to the Orient never formed a nation. They did not found a new homeland. They were a mere handful of temporary rulers, officials and traders protected by a garrison. When their work was done, or their fortune made, they retired to the land of their birth.

The Whites who settled at the foot of Africa three hundred years ago were colonists. They never returned to Europe. They retained no ties with the land from which they came. They evolved a language used nowhere else on the globe. Today the majority of the Whites in South Africa were born there. They know no other land. They feel they must remain as rulers or ruled.

Nor did the Whites who made their home at the foot of Africa nearly three centuries ago settle on the lands of the Black peoples whose leaders now raise the cry of Africa for the Africans. They began to colonize the Cape while the Bantu tribes were a thousand miles away.

White settlement was begun by the Dutch East India Company in April, 1652. It needed a refreshment station from which water, meat and vegetables could be supplied to its ships trading with the East. Commander Van Riebeeck built a fort and planted a garden. He found an almost empty land containing only wandering bands of Hottentots and Bushmen seeking pasture for their cattle. The warlike tribes known for many years as the Kafirs (or Caffres)— now called the Bantu, or the Africans, or the Natives—were then moving down the far distant east coast of the sub-continent. The

Dutch at the Cape did not come into contact with them for a hundred years.

The Company's garden however did not produce enough for the ships. In order to stimulate cultivation the Company in 1657 gave nine of their employees letters of discharge authorising them to settle as independent farmers in the vicinity of the fort. Their number was gradually increased and they became the founders of White South Africa.

The Hottentots and Bushmen however had no wish to work as labourers for the newcomers; and Van Riebeeck suggested that slaves should be imported. The Company agreed, and the first batches of Negroes from the West coast of Africa were landed in 1658. Other slaves were brought in from the East Indies, Madagascar and East Africa, and when slavery was finally abolished there were found to be 29,021 slaves at the Cape. Their descendants became the Cape Coloured people who played a considerable part in the development of the country.

The policy of placing 'free burghers' (as they were called) on the land was successful, and for a time immigration from Europe was also encouraged and by 1688 there were nearly six hundred freemen settled on the soil. Their number was swollen by the arrival of two hundred Huguenots who had fled from France to escape religious persecution. The French families were rapidly absorbed into the community of free Hollanders and Germans who began to be known as the Boers (farmers) although they preferred to be called Afrikanders (later spelt Afrikaners) to indicate they were not merely servants of the East Indian Company.

In his social and economic history of South Africa, Professor C. W. de Kiewiet remarked that 'there were few compelling reasons, and no climatic reasons, why the Dutch and the Huguenots could not have remained a truly White society'. Indeed, had diamonds and gold been discovered in the seventeenth or eighteenth century instead of the nineteenth the history of South Africa might have borne more resemblance to that of North America or Australia. There would have been a rush of Europeans into a thinly peopled land with a climate eminently suitable for White colonization. The foot of Africa might have become mainly a White man's land.

In the seventeenth and eighteenth centuries however South Africa offered no attraction to the trading nations. It appeared to be a vast country inhabited by savages with no economic potentialities.

Even the Directors of the East India Company became dissatisfied
with the progress of their Cape settlement. In 1717 they called
upon the Council of Policy at the Cape to report what could be
done to make it more useful.

Among other things, the Directors asked whether European
farm-hands would not be better than slaves—whether the settlement should be based upon free White labour or upon servile
Coloured labour. 'Probably,' wrote Theal, the historian of the
Boers, 'no subject of equal importance has ever since engaged the
attention of the authorities, for upon these reports was to depend
whether the country should be occupied solely by Europeans or
whether there would be a mixture of races in it.'

With one exception the members of the Council of Policy
expressed a preference for Coloured labour. The majority condemned White labour as lazy and incompetent and more expensive
than slave labour.

The only man who defended free labour was Dominique de
Chavonnes, the captain of the garrison and a brother of the
Governor. He was whole-heartedly in favour of European immigrants. He declared that the colony could absorb White artisans;
and even if the Europeans had to be paid £12 a year, against the
£6 that had to be paid for a slave, two Whites would do the work
of three Coloured men and would give the colony the advantage
of husbands for the women and a defence force that would enable
the Company to reduce the size of the garrison of professional
soldiers. Pressure of population would also, he argued, compel the
Whites to work harder and develop the resources of the country
by making it a land of small farms instead of large plantations.
De Chavonnes told his colleagues that 'two hundred and fifty
pioneers will be of more use, and more profitable to the Company,
than five or six hundred slaves, male, female and children.'

De Chavonnes was defeated; yet in later years Van Imhoff, who
visited the Cape on his way to become Governor-General of the
Dutch East Indies, confessed that he had been right. 'I believe,'
he said, 'it would have been better had we, when this colony was
founded, commenced with Europeans and brought them hither
in such numbers that hunger and want would have forced them to
work. But having imported slaves, every common or ordinary
European becomes a gentleman and prefers to be served than to
serve. We have in addition the fact that the majority of the farmers
in this country are not farmers in the real sense of the word but

plantation owners, and many of them consider it a shame to work with their hands.'

Relying upon slaves for the cultivation of the soil, the Dutch East India Company pursued a policy of non-intercourse with the tribes in the hinterland. The free burghers, however, who were moving farther and farther inland, began to employ Hottentots as farm labourers and servants. There were sometimes clashes with them, and with the Bushmen; yet White occupation extended far into the interior with very little opposition from the local tribes. The Kafirs were still far away and European authority was not seriously challenged.

In the first days of the rule of the Dutch East India Company there was practically no discrimination on the ground of the colour of the skin. A profession of Christianity was considered sufficient to place White and Black more or less on the same level. A baptized Black enjoyed virtually the rights and privileges of a European. There were even a few marriages between Europeans and Hottentots.

With the increased use of slave labour public opinion underwent a change. Soon it was held to be a disgrace for a European to marry a person of colour. In 1685 the marriage of Europeans with freed slaves of full colour was banned, although Whites and half-breeds were allowed to marry.

As the number of free burghers increased the feeling against a mixture of blood grew stronger. By the middle of the eighteenth century the Whites in South Africa regarded colour very much as did the Whites in America. Abraham Lincoln, who abolished slavery in the United States, was conscious of this feeling. He said, even as late as 1854, that he would not hold the Negro in slavery: but he added: 'What next? Free them and make them politically and socially our equals? My own feelings will not permit of this: and if mine would we know well that those of the great mass of the Whites will not. Whether this feeling accords with justice and sound judgment is not the whole question, if indeed it is any part of it. A universal feeling, whether well or ill-founded, cannot safely be disregarded. We cannot make them our equal.'

Four years later the Great Emancipator supported a colour bar. He said that he had never advocated the social and political equality of White and Black. He declared he was not in favour of giving the franchise to Negroes, or of admitting them to public office, or of allowing marriages between them and the Whites.

That was also the attitude of the Afrikaners, as indeed it was of the majority of northern Europeans at that period. They had no wish to exercise control over the tribes in the interior or to have anything to do with them. They did not regard the Natives as potential fellow-citizens but as separate peoples having their own homelands. The Dutch East India Company warned its servants not to make contacts with the tribesmen, and it included the Kafirs (the Bantu) among the people with whom the burghers were to have no intercourse.

The Dutch Governors at the Cape insisted that there must be no expansion into Kafir country. Governor van Plettenberg, in 1774, issued an edict threatening to fine, or even to condemn to death, anyone who persisted in trafficking with the Natives. He made a long and trying journey to the frontier in 1788 to try by his personal authority to prevent intercourse with the tribesmen. In the same year the Council of Policy ratified a treaty by which the Fish River, some six hundred miles from Cape Town, was made the dividing line between the Whites and the Bantu. This early attempt at segregation failed, for the Xosas crossed the river again and their incursion led to the first of the many so-called Kafir Wars.

The foundations of the White race that established itself in a Black continent were laid by a people of Dutch, German and French descent who formed the composite race long known as the South African Dutch. A people isolated mentally as well as geographically, they revealed the virtues and faults that sprang from their peculiar environment. Self-reliant, highly individualistic and fanatically independent, they developed a passionate love of their country and its ways and resented the slightest interference by strangers. O. F. Mentzel, a German who travelled widely in the Cape, wrote of them: 'If one should speak of the advantages that Europe offered over the African lands they are at once prone to ask why the speaker did not stay at home and enjoy them'.

The Dutch East India Company ruled the Cape for nearly a hundred and fifty years. It is doubtful whether it could have held its authority indefinitely. A rift was opening between the officials at the Castle and the free burghers who were moving farther and farther inland and becoming more and more resentful of the monopolistic methods of the Directors in the Netherlands. Like the colonial-born people in Britain's oversea possessions they were beginning to chafe at control from a distant capital.

The Company had no opportunity of showing whether it could satisfy colonial demands for self-government. Its rule ended abruptly. In 1795, when the French revolutionary armies overran the Netherlands, a British fleet seized the Cape in the name of the exiled Stadholder. A change in the European kaleidoscope in 1803 brought the Batavian Republic into existence, and the British returned the Cape to it. In its short life the Republican regime planned to send out more people from Europe to strengthen the White population, but it did not prohibit the importation of slaves. In any case it had no time to develop a new policy. In 1806 the war broke out again and the British occupied the Cape for the second time and kept it as one of the outposts of empire essential to the protection of their trade with the East Indies. In the general settlement after peace the British Government paid the Netherlands £6,000,000 for the loss of the territory.

Great Britain took over an African land twice the size of England. It contained 25,000 Europeans, who ruled 30,000 slaves and 20,000 Hottentots. There were only fifty or sixty British people in the colony.

The entry of the British brought another White race into South Africa and began a struggle for supremacy with the older population that lasted for nearly a hundred years. Incidentally, it introduced different ideas about the treatment of the Non-White population and so laid the seeds of another conflict the outcome of which is still uncertain.

CHAPTER II

Early Colour Policy

By acquiring the Cape, Great Britain took over a mainly Dutch settlement. Transfers of territories with their inhabitants were not uncommon in those days. Pride of race had not become the fiery sentiment that led someone to describe the nineteenth century as 'the age of nationalism'.

At first the change was accepted without rancour. Economically the Dutch at the Cape benefitted by the change. The maintenance of British troops and ships provided a larger local market, while the preference granted by Great Britain to Cape wines gave the farmers a period of unexampled prosperity; wine exports became greater than all other exports put together.

Moreover the articles of capitulation laid down that the burghers were to retain all the rights and privileges they had enjoyed under the Batavian Republic. The Boers found themselves governed under their old laws and largely by local officials they knew.

The British Governors were Tories whose ideas were acceptable to a land-owning class. They had no revolutionary notions about the equality of Black and White. When the Cape was first occupied in 1795, the military Governor, the Earl of Macartney, issued a proclamation excluding all Kafirs from the colony, and a few years later Governor Sir S. F. Craddock drove them back over the Fish River.

In 1807 Great Britain abolished slavery, and no more slaves could be shipped to the Cape. As farming was expanding, this led to a shortage of labour on the land. The Hottentots were not willing to work, and the authorities were asked to bring pressure upon them to induce them to work for the Europeans. So in 1809 the first civil Governor, the Earl of Caledon, introduced a pass law for Hottentots. Under it all the males not working for Whites were classified as 'vagrants'. Any Hottentot who was a vagrant could be punished unless he carried a pass, and every White man, not only the police, had the right to stop a Hottentot and ask to see his pass.

But the only way by which a Hottentot could obtain a pass was to enter into a labour agreement with a White farmer, though the law did not lay down any rate of pay and the wage offered was very small. Hottentots who did not enter into labour agreements were arrested for being without a pass and were hired out among the farmers. There was also a system by which the children of Hottentots could be apprenticed to farmers; and the missionaries denounced it as child slavery.

The amicable relations between the two White races began to fade when British policy underwent a change after the number of British in the colony was substantially increased.

Although Great Britain emerged triumphant in the Napoleonic Wars there was much unemployment in the country. State emigration schemes were launched to relieve the increasing distress. Canada was preferred by the majority of the potential emigrants, though Lord Bathurst told those who thought of seeking their fortune in a new land: 'The Cape of Good Hope, from the fertility of the soil and the superiority of the climate, affords the greater facilities for the establishment of a settlement'.

At that time the British Government could have turned the racial balance in South Africa in favour of the English. Some ninety thousand people applied for passages to the Cape, yet the Government sent out only five thousand men, women and children, who were known as the 1820 Settlers.

The arrival of the immigrants introduced a large body of Whites who brought their own language and traditions from a distant land to which they continued to turn for their culture and inspiration. Backed by reinforcements of their own race, the British Governors grew less considerate of the feelings and prejudices of the older population. They began to try to convert the Cape into a typical English colony, and in 1832 English was made the only language used in the courts.

The missionary societies in Britain saw a new field for activity in South Africa, and their agents were imbued with the new spirit of humanitarianism and liberalism that was beginning to influence society and administration in England. The mission churches in the Cape entered strong protests against the laws discriminating against 'free persons of colour'. In 1828 the Cape Government proclaimed Ordinance 50 which abolished all the earlier restrictive laws affecting the Hottentots passed since 1809. The new law did not cover the slaves held in the colony, but it applied to all other Non-Whites. It declared:

> 'As is has been the custom of this colony for Hottentots and other free persons of colour to be subject to certain hindrances as to their place of living, way of life and employment, and to certain forced services which do not apply to other subjects of His Majesty, be it therefore made law that from and after the passing of this Ordinance no Hottentot or other free person of colour lawfully living in this colony shall be subject to any forced service which does not apply to others of His Majesty's subjects, nor to any hindrances, interference, fine or punishment of any kind whatever under the pretence that such person has been guilty of vagrancy or any other offence unless after trial in the due course of law, any custom or usage to the contrary notwithstanding.'

The Ordinance gave the Hottentots the right to buy land, and laid down that in future any labour agreement of over one month must be in writing.

The 1828 Ordinance did not alter the position of the slaves; but in 1834 slavery was abolished within the British Empire. The slave-holders in the Cape were on the whole content to end the system; but of the £20 millions set aside for compensating the owners of slaves in the British Empire only £1,247,000 was allotted to the Cape, and then all the claims had to be proved in London. In the end the Cape slave-owners received only one-fifth of the value of their slaves instead of the one-third they had expected. The farmers complained too that no vagrancy law was passed to control the movements of the liberated slaves, who became 'free persons of colour' and were able to wander about the country as they pleased. By another law all Non-Europeans were given the same rights in the courts as the Europeans.

The Dutch East India Company's policy of non-intercourse with the Kafirs was abandoned, and they were accepted as part of the population of the colony. In 1834 some seventeen thousand Fingoes, who were good farm workers, were placed between the Fish and Kei Rivers as a sort of buffer against the more warlike tribes. Reserves and locations were marked out for exclusive occupation by Natives so that European settlers placed on the frontier would be able to draw labour from them.

The Dutch became more and more resentful of British methods, and from 1834 onwards began to move out of the colony in the exodus known as the Great Trek, until some ten thousand had taken their departure.

Sir Benjamin D'Urban, the Governor of the Cape from 1834 to 1838, wrote that the causes of the Trek were 'insecurity of life and property occasioned by the recent measures, inadequate compensation for the loss of slaves, and despair of obtaining recompense for ruinous losses of the Kafir invasion.'

Mrs. Anna Steenkamp, a sister of Piet Retief, one of the leaders of the Trek, writing forty years afterwards, said that the chief reason for the exodus was that slaves 'were placed on an equal footing with Christians contrary to the laws of God and the natural distinction of race and colour, so that it was intolerable for any decent Christian to bow down beneath such a yoke: therefore we rather withdrew in order to preserve our doctrines in purity.'

An effort was made to persuade the Trekkers to stay. Sir Benjamin D'Urban spoke of them as 'brave, patient, industrious, orderly and religious people, the cultivators, defenders and tax contributors of the country.'

But those who had decided to go would not change their mind. They believed that they would find more and better land in the interior, and they were determined to rule themselves and maintain the colour bar which was weakening in the Cape under British sovereignity.

The Great Trek had an unfortunate influence upon the politico-racial development of South Africa. Had the two peoples remained under one system of government they might gradually have formed a united nation. They might have moved into the interior together without dividing the sub-continent into separate and often hostile States. The Great Trek widened the gap between them. The interior became almost exclusively Afrikaans, and the coast increasingly British.

Thus throughout the nineteenth century South Africa was distracted by the rivalry between Briton and Boer. The conflict overshadowed the problem of the co-existence of White and Non-White during a formative period in which a sustained and united effort to strengthen the White race would have placed the colour question of a more manageable basis. By a vigorous immigration policy the numerical disparity between Europeans and Non-Europeans could have been greatly reduced. In the Cape Colony in 1863 the Whites were outnumbered by the Non-Whites by fewer than two to one. In the Orange Free State in 1880 there were 61,000 Whites to only 72,000 Non-Whites. In Natal the Whites had always been greatly outnumbered by the Blacks and unhappily from 1860 the colour problem was rendered more complicated by the importation of large numbers of Indians.

In those days however very little attention was paid to the question of the future co-existence of Whites and Non-Whites. There were no misgivings regarding the position of the Whites. Imperial troops protected the British colonies. The mass of the Natives accepted the place allotted to them in the community. The basic problem in the sub-continent was held to be one of race —Afrikaners versus British—and not one of colour.

In any case the rift between Briton and Boer made it more and more difficult to frame a common policy in dealing with the Non-Whites.

The Boers who trekked into the interior finally established republics whose constitutions were based on the principle that there must be no equality between Black and White.

In the Cape on the other hand the colour bar was fading and the Non-Whites were given a voice in local government.

In Natal the Trekkers had established the Republic of Natalia with its capital at Pietermaritzburg. Its Volksraad passed a resolution ordering that all the Natives found in the republic were to be removed into 'a country between the rivers Umtaphoons and Umzimbuvu', forming part of Pondoland. The Volksraad declared the measure 'proceeded from real practical philanthropy to avoid collisions of different races, which would inevitably result from the continued residence of themselves and the Natives.'

But the British Special Commissioner, the Hon. Henry Cloete, read to the Volksraad a despatch from the British Secretary of State for the Colonies setting out the conditions under which the Trek Boers would be allowed to stay in Natal. One condition was that 'there shall not be in the eyes of the law any distinction of colour, origin, language or creed'. The Boers had to accept the condition for the moment; though when Great Britain formally annexed Natal in 1845 most of them left the colony and moved into the Boer republics.

Natal developed a Non-White policy that differed from that of the Cape Colony. Thus there emerged three different ways of dealing with Non-Whites.

The Cape Colony became an experimental station for more liberal ideas. Even in 1836 its Legislative Council had set up municipal boards in the towns and villages and allowed persons of colour to vote in the elections for them. In Cape Town a Coloured man was appointed a wardmaster. When representative government was granted to the colony in 1853 its Legislative Council asked for a rather high qualification for the electorate. The British Government lowered it on the ground that it was undesirable that the franchise should be so restricted as to leave practically unrepresented those of the Coloured class who in point of intelligence were qualified for the exercise of political power. Explaining this policy, the British Colonial Office stated that it was the desire of the British Government that all Her Majesty's subjects at the Cape 'without distinction of class or colour' should be united in one bond of loyalty and a common interest, and that the Government believed that 'the exercise of political rights enjoyed by all alike would prove one of the best methods of attaining this object'.

When the Cape constitution was promulgated there were few Bantu within the borders of the colony and the franchise embraced mainly Europeans and Coloureds. In 1886 however a change in the franchise law enabled the Bantu in the recently annexed Transkeian territories to qualify on the usual terms, and the cry went up that the 'blanket Kafirs' were getting on the register and that it was even proposed to put up a Kafir as a candidate. At once the Parliamentary Registration Bill was introduced. It struck off the roll a large number of Natives whose registration was found to be doubtful. It also declared that 'no person shall be entitled to be registered as a voter by reason of his sharing in any communal or tribal occupation of land or buildings'. This meant that a Native would have to own property to the value of £25 or more on individual freehold tenure before he could qualify to be registered. J. H. ('Onze Jan') Hofmeyr, the founder and leader of the Afrikaner Bond, supported the measure. He believed in Native representation but felt that the Natives who then wielded this power were to a great extent sunk in barbarism. He wanted civilization and not colour to be the test for the franchise.

The Registration Bill was passed by a big majority, and it resulted in some thirty thousand Bantu being struck off the voters' roll.

The non-White vote in the Cape continued to increase, and in 1892 the Rhodes Ministry put through Parliament a franchise

Act which raised the property qualification from £25 to £75 and laid down that every applicant for registration as a voter must be able to sign his name in the presence of the registering officer. This educational test did not have the desired effect, for the agents of the political parties arranged classes in which Natives and Coloureds were taught to write their names and assisted to get on the voters' roll.

At the 1893 general election in the Cape it was reported that the very considerable Malay community meant to nominate a man of Turkish descent named Attoam Mah Effendi. At that time there was a form of proportional representation called the cumulative vote. Several large constituencies returned more than one member and every voter was allowed as many votes as there were candidates on the voting paper. The voter could if he wished give all his votes to one candidate only. It was said that the Malays proposed to give all their votes to Attoam Mah and thus secure his return.

Before election day, however, the Legislature rushed through the Constitutional Amendment Bill which abolished the cumulative vote. 'Onze Jan' Hofmeyr was the only member opposing the Bill. He said that his objection to colour was not so strong that he would object to a well-educated man like the Effendi sitting in that House, and if he himself was returned the Effendi was welcome to sit beside him.

Hofmeyr always denied that the Afrikaner Bond wanted to deprive the Kafir of his vote. 'What the Bond wants,' he said, 'is that the franchise should not be so arranged that we are delivered politically into the hands of a troop of barbarians, the sport of speculating agents or prejudiced missionaries.' He added that the Bond was also accused of wanting to keep the Natives uneducated, stupid and ignorant. The Bond, he declared, was for education 'but for such education as will fit those educated for their position in society, for the calling that Providence has provided for them. The Bond desires that that principle should be applied not only to Kafirs but to Whites.'

While the Cape Colony had been adopting a more liberal attitude on the colour question, Natal had been enforcing another policy. It had been framed by Theophilus Shepstone, a missionary's son who had been brought up among the Xosas in the eastern part of the Cape and had become the head of the Native Affairs Department in Natal. He rejected the idea of equality favoured by

the missionaries. He believed in segregation and racial differentiation. The Natives were to live in their own areas, governed as far
as possible through their own chiefs under Native law, though
cases involving Whites were to be dealt with in White courts.
He established eight Native Reserves covering over a million acres
with a population of eighty thousand. Shepstone wished to guide
the Natives to progress through the institutions to which they
were accustomed. He was an early creator of Bantustans.

In 1856 Natal was given a Legislative Council in which twelve
members were to be elected. The qualification which entitled a
person to vote or to become a member of the Council made no
reference to race and placed the franchise within the reach of every
British subject irrespective of the colour of his skin.

In 1865, however, the Natal Legislature altered the franchise by
a law that laid down the first statutory colour bar enacted in a
British colony in South Africa. The Natives in Natal were subject
to special laws, and the new law excluded from the franchise
Natives who, although possessing the qualifications laid down,
were still governed by special laws. This measure practically disfranchised the entire Native population of Natal, although
Coloureds or other Non-Europeans could become voters.

The Boers who trekked into the interior pursued yet another
policy. They would have nothing to do with Cape ideas.

In 1848 British sovereignity was proclaimed over the territory
lying between the Orange and Vaal Rivers, and it was laid down
that the rights and privileges existing in the Cape Colony would be
extended to the people of the territory. This meant that there would
be no colour bar under British rule. But in 1854 the Orange Free
State was given independence, and it immediately adopted a constitution conferring franchise rights upon White persons only. One
of its laws declared: 'No Arab, Chinaman or Coolie or other
Asiatic Coloured person may settle in the State for longer than
two months without permission.'

The Boers in the Transvaal enforced the same policy. The
constitution of their republic stated: 'The people will permit no
equality between White and Coloured inhabitants, either in Church
or State.' Residential segregation was ordered in another article
which read: 'No Natives shall be allowed to establish their residence
near towns to the detriment of the inhabitants except with the
permission of the full Raad.'

The Transvaal also introduced a pass system in the instructions issued to Field Cornets on September 17, 1859; though the first legislative enactment was Law 9 of 1860 which laid down that every male Native must carry a pass issued by his master, a missionary, landdrost, field cornet or chief. It stated that passes were required 'owing to the large number of rootless Natives roaming about the country'. The pass was issued 'for the protection of those Natives desiring permanent residence and employment', and the holders of such passes were 'entitled to the full protection of the law and the Government like any other subject'.

The British annexed the Transvaal in 1877, and the proclamation announcing the fact declared that 'equal justice is guaranteed to the persons and property of both Whites and persons of Colour; but the adoption of this principle does not, and should not, involve the granting of equal civil rights such as the exercise of the right of voting by savages, or their becoming members of a legislative body, or their being entitled to other civil privileges which are incompatible with their uncivilized condition.'

After the South African Republic was re-established in the Transvaal in 1881 the colour bar was restored, and a law of 1896 declared: 'The people will not permit the equalization of persons of colour with White inhabitants.'

The Boer principle was explained by President Kruger in 1888. He said: 'The missionaries seem often to have failed to understand that for the Boers the Native question is necessarily not only a religious and humanitarian question but also a political question.... The Boers are neither opposed to the missionaries nor are enemies of the Natives. Their principle is to allot a certain district to every tribe that keeps quiet and peaceful and is willing to accept civilization, such district to be in proportion to the size of the tribe.'

The Kruger Government appointed a commission to mark out Reserves for the Bantu; but owing to increasing disputes with the British Government there was no attempt to fix boundary lines.

While the Whites in the Cape and the two republics were devising ways of dealing with the Bantu and the Coloureds the settlers in Natal introduced yet another race to complicate the situation in South Africa. They had been experimenting with the production of tea and sugar and found that the Zulu labour at their door was unsatisfactory. They cast longing eyes at Mauritius, where a flourishing sugar industry had been built up on the basis of Indian labour. They too wanted 'coolies'; and when Sir George Grey visited Natal the Durban Corporation presented an address asking for sanction for the introduction of 'a limited number of coolie or other labourers from the East in aid of the new enterprises on the coast lands to the success of which sufficient and reliable labour is absolutely essential.'

Sir George Grey was impressed and told the Colonial Secretary in London that the use of Indian labour would promote the wealth of the colony and 'render it of value and importance to Great Britain'. The British Government sanctioned the importation of Indians under contract, and the first shipment of 'coolie labour' reached Durban in November 1860. There were then only seven thousand Europeans in Natal; but in the next twelve years thirty thousand Indians were allowed to enter and the censuses of 1904 and 1911 showed that the Asiatics in the colony outnumbered the Whites.

When Natal was granted responsible government in 1893 one of its first acts was to pass a franchise law which laid down that in future male immigrants and their descendants who came from countries where they did not enjoy the parliamentary franchise would not be included in the voters' roll. Thus without mentioning Indians, the Indians were deprived of the vote. The further entry of free Indians was also prohibited; and as a reprisal the Indian Government stopped the further recruiting of indentured labour for Natal.

Natal's policy made the colour question more troublesome in other parts of South Africa. At first its Indians were content to remain in the coastal belt. As they increased in numbers, however, they moved inland. The Cape was too far away and they began to infiltrate into the two Boer republics.

The Government of the Orange Free State promptly passed a law excluding them. The Transvaal would have liked to follow suit; but it was bound by Article XIV of the London Convention of 1884, which provided that all persons other than Natives were to have full liberty to reside and trade and own property in any part of the republic.

The Indians who entered the Transvaal were traders, and before long an agitation sprang up—initiated by the Chambers of Commerce in which the English element predominated—in favour of placing restrictions upon Indian trading. To meet the wishes of the White shopkeepers, President Kruger approached the British Government for permission to pass legislation preventing the further infiltration of Indians. He proposed to do so by the simple method of interpreting the term 'Natives' in the London Convention to include Asiatics. The British Government rejected the request, though it intimated that it was not unwilling 'for sanitary reasons' to sanction legislation compelling Asiatics to live in bazaars or locations, with the proviso that British Indians of the trader class should be left entirely free. The Kruger Government thereupon passed Law 3 of 1885 which made the registration of Asiatics compulsory, debarred them from the franchise, and prohibited them from holding land except in areas specially demarcated. The Indians protested loudly against the law and it was never enforced.

The London Convention had secured for 'Natives' in the Transvaal access to the courts of law, and freedom to move within the country or to leave it under a pass system. The Kruger Government however classed Cape Coloureds and other coloured British subjects, many of whom had a good deal of European blood in their veins, as 'Natives'. They were compelled to take out passes and to wear badges and were not allowed to walk on the side-pavements. The British Agent in Pretoria protested against this treatment; but the question was a difficult one as the interpretation of the term 'Natives' in the Convention was not made clear at the time the agreement was signed.

The general treatment of Non-Whites was not, however, regarded as a major issue in South Africa in the closing years of the nineteenth century. The fundamental issue was held to be the relations between the Afrikaners and the British. Sir Alfred Milner was sent out as High Commissioner in May, 1897, to try to secure better treatment for the British and other Outlanders in the Transvaal. It was his chief task, yet he soon arrived at the conclusion that the relations between Black and White were of greater moment.

In one of his letters he said that Lady Hanbury Williams, who acted as hostess at Government House, had 'kissed a Black child as well as a White', an incident which led to a good deal of criticism of British ways. After explaining what had happened, Milner went on : 'I think she was right. Most White people in South Africa think she was wrong. There you have the great South African problem posed at once. It is the Native question. The Anglo-Dutch friction is bad enough. But it is child's play compared with the antagonism of White and Black. That the White man must rule is clear—but HOW? That is the point where my views and those of most Englishmen differ radically from those of most Colonials. And this and not the Dutch Business is the subject with respect to which I foresee the greatest difficulty.'

In a confidential letter to Mr. Asquith in November, 1897, Milner said that if the Imperial Government were to be seen taking a strong line for the protection of the Blacks both British and Dutch opinion in the sub-continent would swing round against it.

'You have therefore,' continued Milner, 'this singular situation, that you might unite Dutch and English by protecting the Black man, but you would unite them against yourself and your policy of protection. There is the whole CRUX of the South African position. . . . By far the worst is the Transvaal. Here the Black has no rights whatever and there is neither kindness nor wisdom to restrain the brutality of the ruling oligarchy. In contrast . . . is the position of the Black man in Basutoland and the Bechuanaland Protectorate. Here there is absolute protection for the Black man against oppression and wrong . . . But look at the result. The Imperial position in Basutoland and the Bechuanaland Protectorate is a source of constant friction with the Colonials . . . I want to preserve the Basuto and the Bechuana for the present at least from the tender mercies of the Bond and our friend Cecil J. Rhodes. But observe that by doing so I am weakening my hand in the game of conciliating the Colonials, Dutch and English, and uniting Dutch and English. Dutch and English in the Colony are united in wanting to take over Basutoland. Even the Dutch would like to see Rhodes pocket the Bechuanaland Protectorate . . . They hate Rhodes for the moment—but they hate an independent Native State more—and at all times.'

Milner's negotiations with Kruger failed, and the South African War began in October 1899, and lasted for two years and eight months. In 1900 the British Government annexed the Transvaal and the Orange Free State. The Treaty of Vereeniging was signed on May 31, 1902. The eighth clause of the Treaty read:

'The question of granting the franchise to Natives will not be decided until after the introduction of self-government.'

The Treaty did not forbid the franchise being extended to Coloured people and Asians.

CHAPTER III

Colour Bars under British Rule

In the opening years of the twentieth century most of South
Africa was manifestly British. The two Boer republics had gone.
There were now four British colonies in which the flying of the
Union Jack and the singing of 'God Save the Queen' denoted
close association with the Mother Country.

Milner was trying to persuade the Boers to work under British
institutions. His staff was composed largely of young civil servants
and was known as 'the Kindergarten'. His aim, as he told a friend,
was 'to give South Africa a preponderatingly, but not of course an
exclusive, British character'. He wished to build up a united
nation; but he wanted to do it by transforming the Boers into good
Britishers. As one of his interpreters put it, his object was 'the
triumph under self-government of British political ideals'.

The political future of the Boers was not however the immediate
issue after the Peace of Vereeniging. The first task was to fit the
ex-republics into the framework of British South Africa. In the
controversies that had preceded the war it had been suggested that
under British rule radical changes would be made, especially on the
colour question, to bring the Transvaal and the Orange Free State
more into line with the British system. In the event, British policy
differed little from that of the Boers.

At first, the Transvaal was governed as a Crown Colony. Its
nominated Legislative Council drafted an Ordinance providing for
the election of a Town Council for Johannesburg. It extended the
franchise to every person possessing a specified property qualification irrespective of racial origin or colour. The unofficial
members of the legislature promptly protested against the omission
of a colour bar. The Government could, of course, have passed the
Ordinance as it was drafted; yet it yielded to the wishes of the

28

public and the measure was amended and all non-Europeans were excluded from the polling booths. In the Orange Free State (then the Orange River Colony) a similar Ordinance also contained a colour bar.

During the war, promises had been made that under British rule the Indians and the Cape Coloureds in the republics would be treated in the same way as those in the Cape, where they had equal rights with the Europeans in the holding of property, trading, freedom of locomotion, the franchise and so on. So the fifteen thousand Indians who had left the Transvaal on the outbreak of hostilities streamed back expecting to live in future under more liberal conditions.

But again Milner found that he could not apply the policy that had been suggested by distant idealists. The pattern of South African life could not easily be altered. The enactments of the Kruger regime were not swept away; and the Indians complained that their position was 'worse than before the war'. In India, Sir Henry Cotton, the President of the Indian National Congress, felt constrained to say: 'The British rulers of the Transvaal have applied themselves with vigour and precision to the task of enforcing Boer law. In dealing with Indian colonists their little finger has been thicker than Mr. Kruger's loins, and where he had whips they have chastised with scorpions.'

The British Administration did not remove the colour bar in the gold mines. It made no basic change in the treatment of the Natives. In Pretoria a by-law compelling the Blacks to walk in the roadway and not on the side-walks was not rescinded until 1912. Milner and his lieutenants had to admit that they could not defy popular feeling.

In a despatch in 1904, Sir Arthur Lawley, the Lieutenant-Governor of the Transvaal, put the position very frankly. He wrote: 'I do not seek to justify the [colour] prejudices which exist: I merely desire to set them forth. They cannot be ignored. It is true that the British Government have laid down that there shall not be in the eyes of the law any distinction or disqualification whatever founded on mere distinction of colour, origin, language or creed: but the history of South Africa has been such as to set up an impassable barrier between the European and Coloured races. The introduction and establishment of a White race in this country has only been effected after constant warfare with savage tribes who have from time to time rebelled against the domination of the

White man. These outbreaks have invariably been accompanied by murders and outrages of a revolting description of which many men now living have been actual eye-witnesses. These episodes cannot be effaced from the memory of any South Africans and have engendered a feeling of animosity against the Coloured man which cannot be eradicated by legislation . . . Under the old Grondwet the line was distinctly drawn between Coloured and White; and though in the eyes of the law they are equal, there is not in this country one man in a hundred who would agree to recognise the Coloured man as capable of admission to the same social standard as the White. I do not urge that these sentiments are reasonable; but they imbue the mind of every South African and find expression in the universal cry of "A White Man's Country". The result of any attempt to ignore them would be attended, I feel sure, with most deplorable results.'

Lord Milner himself, in a despatch to Mr. Lyttelton, the Secretary of State for the Colonies, in April, 1904, wrote: 'I think that to attempt to place Coloured people on an equality with Whites in South Africa is wholly impracticable and that moreover it is in principle wrong. But I hold also that when a Coloured man possesses a certain high grade of civilization he ought to obtain what I call "White privileges" irrespective of his colour. I have on more than one occasion given expression to these views. They are very unpopular in the Transvaal at the present time, but I do not despair of their ultimately prevailing.'

Lord Elgin, when Secretary of State for India, confessed to an Indian deputation that there could be found despatches with his signature protesting against restrictions on the ground of colour. 'I do not,' he said, 'go back from one single word. But we have to recognize the fact that there are difficulties arising on the part of the White communities and we have to reckon with them. The fact of there being sentiment has to be borne in mind when we have to deal with matters of this description.'

There was an agitation in favour of the abolition of the Pass Law and the British Government was approached by the Aborigines Protection Society. Milner reported on the subject in the following terms: 'The root idea of the old Pass Law was not a wrong one. If the aboriginal Natives are to come and go in large numbers in search of labour, and are to reside for considerable periods in the midst of a White community, there must be some sort of passport system else the place will be a pandemonium. Alike for the protection of the Natives and the protection of the Whites it is absolutely essential to have some reasonable arrangement by which the incoming Native can be identified and his movements traced. The improvement of the laws is therefore merely a step; it is only sound and honest administration which can make the best of laws of any use.'

Sir Godfrey Lagden, Commissioner of Native Affairs, said: 'I am convinced of the necessity of all Natives being compelled to carry passes as much for the security and protection of themselves as for the White people.'

Milner appointed the South African Native Affairs Commission of 1903–5 on which sat representatives from the British colonies and from Southern Rhodesia and the High Commission Territories. The chairman was Sir Godfrey Lagden. It was a purely English body, and some of its members were subsequently described in the South African Parliament as 'pro-Native men'.

This Commission did not advise the removal of colour bars. It agreed that a pass system was necessary. It recommended that the purchase of land by Natives should be confined to specified areas and declared that the creation of a patchwork quilt of White and Black holdings would 'accentuate feelings of race prejudice and animosity with unhappy results'.

The Commission was unanimous in recommending 'separate voting by Native electors only for a fixed number of members to represent them in the legislature of the country, the number not to be more than sufficient to provide an adequate means for the expression of Native views and the ventilation of their grievances, if any, and not to be regulated by the numerical strength of the Native vote: no Native to vote at the election of any candidate who is to represent Europeans.' The Commission held that the Cape Colony system of a common register led inevitably to racial strife.

The Commissioners stated that if the proposals they made were accepted they looked for the avoidance of racial strife; the freeing of all questions affecting the betterment of the Natives from any consideration of consequent increase in their political power; and the direct representation of Native views by members elected by the Natives themselves and by them alone, 'which had never hitherto been the case'.

In the many discussions regarding the future of the Natives at this period one finds little or no support for a policy of equality.

On the contrary there were friends of the Natives who advocated a larger measure of separation.

The Rev. Charles Bourquin, one of the best known missionaries in Southern Africa, read a paper in Pretoria in 1902 in which he said he favoured keeping the races apart. He alluded to the increasing tension between White and Black and went on: 'If we will avoid disaster I think, as many others, that the best thing for Black and White would be for the Natives to live as much as possible their own life, manage their own affairs, and have their independent institutions under the guidance of sympathetic White administrators. We should touch at as few points as possible— have all over South Africa large areas inhabited entirely by Whites and large areas inhabited by Blacks. But the separation, if possible, if it is not too late, should not be carried out without consulting the Natives.'

Other men with long experience of Africa also favoured the policy which became known many years afterwards as Apartheid. In the last quarter of the nineteenth century one of the acknowledged authorities on the Dark Continent was Sir H. H. Johnston. He had explored the continent with Stanley. He had prepared the way for the colonization of Nyasaland, Kenya and Uganda. In an article in the *Fortnightly Review* in 1902 he said that 'south of the Zambesi the ultimate future of the land is for the White man', and suggested that the Blacks should be moved gradually to the tropical regions of the continent.

The British Administration in the Transvaal after the Boer War could not, however, look very far ahead. The immediate task was to get the economic machinery, dislocated by the war, going again. The chief difficulty was that there was not enough labour to restore normal production on the gold mines. The Labour Commission of 1902 reported that there was a shortage of 129,000 Native labourers and that by the end of 1908 there was likely to be a shortage of 250,000. It recommended the importation of Chinese labour under contract. The necessary legislation was passed and the first batch of Chinese reached the Rand in June 1904. The introduction of the Chinese was strongly opposed both in the Transvaal and England and was one of the causes of the defeat of the Unionist Government in Great Britain which enabled a Liberal Government to grant full responsible government to the Transvaal and the Orange Free State.

In the Transvaal the Boer party called Het Volk, led by General

Botha and General Smuts, came into power in 1907. The new
Government soon found itself involved in a struggle arising from
its colour policy.

The nominated Legislative Council which preceded it had
passed a law in 1906 making the carrying of a pass compulsory for
the Indians in the colony. When application was made for the
certificates, thumb-prints had to be given. The Indians protested
and Mahatma Gandhi went to England to ask the British Government to intervene, and the Ordinance was disallowed.

As soon as the Botha Government came into power, however, it
re-imposed the law; and the British Government refused to intervene again on the ground that a self-governing State had the right
to manage its own affairs. The Transvaal Government then
allowed the Indians to register privately in their own homes, but
only about five hundred out of thirteen thousand did so. Gandhi
was arrested for refusing to register and ordered to leave the
country. He would not do so; large numbers of other Indian
resisters were sentenced to imprisonment with hard labour and
soon the jails were filled. The Transvaal's policy was fiercely
denounced in India and gave the colony a bad Press in Great
Britain. Smuts, who as Minister of the Interior was responsible for
the enforcement of the law, then had an interview with Gandhi,
and it was agreed that if the Indians would register voluntarily the
law would be repealed—at least that was what Gandhi understood.

Gandhi resolved to be the first to register and on his way to
do so was attacked by a number of Pathans and severely beaten.
However, the bulk of the Indians registered, only to find that 'the
Black Act', as it was called, was not to be repealed after all. It was
left on the Statute Book to apply to all who had not registered and
to those who entered the Transvaal in the future.

Gandhi called upon the Government to repeal the Act and when
it did not do so the Indians burnt their passes at a mass meeting.
The Government replied with an Immigrants Restriction Act
which made it very difficult for Indians to enter the colony.
Indians from Natal then began to enter the Transvaal and, when
deported, returned again and were sent to prison for three months
with hard labour. The Government struck back by deporting the
resisters to India.

While this struggle was going on in the Transvaal, there was a
serious conflict with the Natives in Natal. The Government there
had imposed a poll tax of £1 per head on every male over the age

of eighteen, irrespective of race or colour. In some areas the Natives refused to pay and the police who were sent in to arrest them were attacked; several were killed. Troops were then used and two soldiers were killed.

In March 1906, twelve Natives were tried by court martial and sentenced to death. The Secretary of State in England instructed the Governor to suspend the carrying out of the sentences. Upon this, the Natal Government resigned. There were strong protests all over South Africa against the interference of the British Government in the affairs of a self-governing colony, and the Australian Government began to ask questions on the matter. On March 31 it was announced that the Imperial Government 'leaves Natal freedom of action regarding the Native executions'. The Natal Government resumed office and the twelve Natives were shot on April 2.

That, however, was not the end of the trouble. A minor chief named Bambata rebelled, and with a considerable force took refuge in the Nkandla forest. Volunteer regiments raised in the Transvaal had by this time arrived in Natal to reinforce the local police and troops, and there was a pitched battle at Mome Gorge in which Bambata and five hundred of his men were killed. The rebellion, which had lasted several months, resulted in nearly four thousand Natives being killed while the Government forces lost twenty-five Europeans and six Natives in the fighting. The poll tax law remained on the Statute Book, though for a long time it was not strictly enforced.

These troubles pointed to the growing difficulty of governing all South Africa with overlordship in London. In 1908 the Natal legislature tried to withdraw trading licences from Asiatics, but the British Government disallowed the measure. There were also financial and economic differences arising from the existence of four separate States, two of which had no access to the sea. In his 'Review of the Present Mutual Relations of the British South African Colonies', Lord Selborne, the Governor-General, declared that the various railway systems were 'absolutely incompatible' and that inter-State railway and custom duties would sooner or later have to be settled 'by arbitration or the sword'.

A liberally financed campaign in favour of union swept the country and the four Colonial Parliaments passed resolutions asking for the calling of a National Convention to draft a federal constitution.

A National Convention was duly summoned and began its sittings in Durban in October, 1908. The main issue was whether the new Dominion was to be federal as in Australia, or strongly unified as in the case of Canada and New Zealand. Mainly owing to the influence of Smuts, the Union of South Africa was created with a centralized government and only Provincial Councils with delegated powers in the former colonies.

There had, however, been some danger of the Union scheme being wrecked on the rock of the non-European vote. In the Cape Colony the Non-European peoples were fully enfranchised and enjoyed the same political rights as the Europeans. In Natal there was no constitutional discrimination between White and non-White though the Natives had been excluded by the law of 1865 and the Indians by the law of 1896. In the Transvaal and the Orange Free State the franchise was confined to the Whites.

Both the political parties in the Cape had vowed that, were the Union formed, there would be no interference with the Coloured vote. At the National Convention sittings, Botha and Smuts for the Transvaal and Abraham Fischer for the Free State suggested that the franchise issue should be left over for the Union Parliament. The Natal delegates, however, insisted that the point should be settled at once, and said they were absolutely opposed to placing the Natives in a position to legislate for White men.

In the end, the Convention decided that the qualification for the franchise should remain in each State as before Union. But it laid down that the members of the Union Parliament must be British subjects of European descent. This removed the right of non-Whites in the Cape to sit in the legislature. The Cape delegates stated that they regretted the colour bar clause in the draft constitution of the Union but they were forced to surrender by the irreconcilable delegates from the northern colonies who declined to enter into union unless non-Whites were barred from membership of the legislature. Section 35 of the South Africa Act, however, provided that 'no voter registered in the province of the Cape of Good Hope may be disqualified by reason of his race or colour only except by a Bill passed at a joint sitting of both Houses of Parliament and at the third reading agreed to by not less than two-thirds of the total members of both Houses.'

The draft constitution drawn up by the National Convention was sent back to the four Colonial Parliaments for their approval. At the Cape, W. P. Schreiner, a strong Liberal, opposed the colour bar and divided the House on it. His amendment was defeated by seventy votes to twenty. He then went to England to try to get the British Parliament to modify the Bill. Several Natives accompanied him. The mission failed to secure any change in the constitution, which had to be accepted unaltered or sent back to be reconsidered in South Africa.

The Natives as a body took no part in the formation of the Union. A small Native Convention met in 1909 to discuss the proposals for uniting the four colonies. Some alterations in the draft constitution were suggested but did not attract attention. The Native Convention appears to have faded away and it was not until three years later that a lasting organization came into being to express Bantu opinion.

'Onze' Jan Hofmeyr, who had fought for the retention of the full Cape franchise in the Union, was thanked by the Coloured People's Vigilance Committee for his efforts. In his reply he wrote: 'With a European population of only a million at the southern extremity of a continent occupied by some two hundred millions, mostly barbarians or semi-barbarians, I cannot help feeling, whatever prejudices of colour and race may be, that the political and social security of White South Africa would be none the worse for retaining the goodwill of the five millions of Coloured and aboriginal inhabitants with whom we live interspersed, and for reconciling them with our political institutions.'

Although the Non-Europeans in the Cape lost their right to sit in the legislature, they were entitled to seek election to the new Provincial Council established in that province.

The Royal instructions to the Governor-General of the Union reserved any Bill disenfranchising any person in the Cape Province from being a voter by reason of race or colour alone. This instruction lasted until 1926 when it was dropped following the resolution passed by the Imperial Conference in that year acknowledging the autonomy of the Dominions.

The South Africa Act provided that the Union was to come into being on May 31, 1910, the eighth anniversary of the signing of the Treaty of Vereeniging. The census taken in the following year showed that the new Dominion began with a total population of 5,973,394 made up of 1,276,242 Europeans, 4,019,006 Natives (Bantu), 152,203 Asians, and 525,943 Coloureds. The non-Whites totalled 4,697,152 and so outnumbered the Whites by roughly three-and-a-half to one.

General Botha was invited to form the first Union Cabinet. There were ten members in it, six of Afrikaner descent and four of British descent. The portfolio of Justice was given to General Hertzog, whose education policy in the Orange Free State had greatly annoyed the British all over South Africa. Thus there was a Union Government in existence, though the Union Parliament had still to be formed.

CHAPTER IV

The Union Accepts Discrimination

In readiness for the first general election in the Union, General Botha formed the South African Party which absorbed the Afrikaner parties in the Cape and the Free State.

Polling day was September 15, 1910, and his party won 67 seats and had a majority of 13 over all the other parties combined. The mainly British Unionist Party, which became the official Opposition, won only 37 seats.

Botha had given the portfolio of Native Affairs to Henry Burton, a well-known barrister who had sat in the old Cape Colony Government. He held the position for little more than a year and did not make any change in Native policy. He put through only one measure, the Native Labour Regulation Act controlling the recruiting and employment of Natives. Its object was to remedy the chaotic conditions under which Natives were recruited for the gold mines. Contractors, labour agents and 'runners' did as they liked, and many Natives were victimized by unfair contracts, overvalued advances and all sorts of deductions from their pay. The old Cape politician, John X. Merriman, tried to get the Government to introduce the Kimberley closed compound system on the Rand gold mines, but Burton refused to enforce it, saying, 'You are trying to introduce a principle which is directly in conflict with the liberty of the subject.'

Early in 1912 there was a crisis in the Cabinet over the railway estimates. It resulted in the resignation of the Minister of Finance, H. C. Hull. A re-shuffle of portfolios followed in which Burton took over Railways and Hertzog became Minister of Native Affairs.

Hertzog took up his new task with his customary thoroughness. He made a careful study of the Native question and arrived at the conclusion that the position was decidedly unsatisfactory.

What are now known as the Native Reserves had been marked out over a long period under varying conditions. In the middle of the nineteenth century the Native population was comparatively small and the allocation of land to different tribes presented little difficulty.

In the Transvaal in 1853 the Commandants of the Republic had been instructed to grant land for occupation by the Bantu, conditional upon good behaviour. The boundaries of these areas were not clearly defined, and under the Pretoria Convention of 1881 a Native Location Commission had been set up to mark out land to which the Bantu were fairly entitled. Owing to the outbreak of the 1899 war the locations were not demarcated until the republic had been taken over by the British.

In the Orange Free State only three Reserves were allotted to the tribes.

In the Cape more separate Native locations had been marked out after the Gaika war of 1877–8; and as other areas were placed under the control of the Cape Government additional locations and reserves were set aside for the tribes.

After Natal had been taken over by the British Government in 1843, locations were demarcated for the Bantu and mission reserves were also marked out, while after the annexation of Zululand an area of nearly four million acres was set aside for the Natives.

By 1910 nearly three hundred Native Reserves, varying in size from a few square miles to a block like the Transkei covering 16,352 square miles, were scattered all over the Union. Large numbers of Natives were also living on land owned by Europeans. Many landowners and land companies were also practising what was called 'Kafir farming' and were allowing Natives to squat on their ground on payment of rent rather than cultivate it themselves. Moreover, all over the Union, except in the Orange Free State, it was legal for Natives to buy or lease land where they liked. In 1912 Natives owned privately some 1,125,000 acres; and there was a strong feeling that the country should not be allowed to become a chequerboard of Black and White settlers.

Faced by this situation Hertzog resolved to deal with it by a policy he called segregation. He said that segregation meant that the Natives would have their own defined areas in which the mass of them would make their homes. Many of them would go out to work for the Whites, but in their own areas they would be able to develop to the full extent of their capacity. He visualized a form of trusteeship which would 'prevent the emergence of a mixed race by miscegenation' and would at the same time save the Natives from 'becoming the prey of what is worst in modern European civilization'.

The basic principle of Hertzog's segregation plan was generally accepted. Smuts had the same idea, though he called it separation. When he was a member of the War Cabinet in England in 1917 he expounded the Union's Native policy in a public speech. He admitted that there were people who did not feel certain that South Africa's White experiment would be a permanent success, or that South Africa could be made a White man's land.

'But,' he added, 'at any rate we shall press on with the experiment. It has now been in progress for some two hundred and fifty years as you know, and perhaps the way we have set about it may be the right way. I am talking of the idea of creating all over South Africa, wherever there is a considerable Native community, independent self-governing institutions for the Native population. Instead of mixing up Black and White in the old way, confusing everything and not lifting up the Black but degrading the White, we are now trying to keep them apart as much as possible in our institutions. In land ownership, in forms of government and in many ways we are trying to keep them apart and thus lay down the outline of a policy which may take a hundred years to work out but which may in the end be the solution of our Native problem. It will certainly be that in South Africa you will have in the long run large areas cultivated by Blacks and governed by Whites where they will look after themselves in all forms of living, and in suitable parts you will have White communities which will govern themselves according to accepted principles. The Natives will come to work in the White areas, but as far as possible the forms of political government will be such that each will be satisfied and developed according to his proper lines. That is the attempt we are now making in South Africa.'

Hertzog, however, disagreed with Botha's policy of conciliating the British and was ejected from the Union Cabinet in 1912 before he could place his plan before Parliament. Yet the Natives Land Bill of 1913 was practically the one he had drafted. It was based upon his idea of segregation. It was the first legislative enactment embodying the principle of territorial segregation and the separation of land rights between Natives and non-Natives. It prohibited the purchase or hire of land by Natives from Europeans and by

Europeans from Natives. It froze temporarily the existing distribution of land. All Native-occupied land was scheduled as Reserves which were to be retained permanently for the exclusive use of the Natives and could not be acquired by Whites. The scheduled Reserves in the Bill covered roughly twenty-five million acres. This however was only a first step. The Bill provided for the appointment of a commission which was to mark out additional areas to be added to the Scheduled Reserves, so that ultimately there would be permanent Native Reserves of adequate size.

The Natives Land Bill was placed before Parliament by J. W. Sauer, a prominent Cape politician who was a Liberal in politics. In his own words the Bill laid down that 'the bulk of the two races, the Europeans and the Natives, should in the main live in separate areas'. He described the measure as 'the Natives Charter with regard to very large areas which will be reserved to them exclusively'.

The Land Bill was supported by the British members in the Union Parliament. B. K. Long, the editor of the *Cape Times*, declared that close association between Black and White was not good. 'If,' he said, 'in South Africa today they could pass a law separating the Whites from the Coloureds they would be doing an inestimable service not only to the future of the Whites but to the future of the Native races.'

H. W. Sampson, a Labour Party member who later became a Cabinet Minister, remarked: 'Why should we single out a few civilized or educated individuals for preferential treatment? The proper place for the educated Native is with his fellows, and he should try to uplift them.'

Sauer claimed in Parliament that the Bill had the support of the well-known Native leader, John Tengo Jabavu, whose organization, called the South African Races Congress, had approved of the principle of the measure, arguing that it was going to give the Natives land and not take it away from them.

The Natives however were divided over the Bill. When the terms of the South Africa Act became known many Natives resented the colour bar in it which banned non-Whites from becoming members of Parliament. Four African lawyers who had studied overseas summoned a convention at Bloemfontein in January 1912, and launched the African National Congress with the object of uniting the Natives in one organization and educating them on their rights and duties and promoting a feeling of brotherhood among them. Among the aims of the Congress was the removal of the colour bar and the securing of the equitable representation of Natives in Parliament.

The African National Congress sent a deputation to London to protest against the Natives Land Bill, but the British Government would not intervene. The Bill was passed by a big majority in the Union Parliament and promptly received the Royal assent.

The Botha Government then appointed a commission under the chairmanship of Sir William Beaumont to report upon what additional land should be 'released' as suitable for the purpose of enlarging the Native Reserves. The commission was to report within two years, though owing to the outbreak of the 1914 World War an extension of twelve months had to be allowed.

In its report, the Beaumont Commission recommended that a further seventeen million acres should be demarcated as suitable for the expansion of the Reserves. This meant that about thirteen per cent of the surface of the Union would finally be reserved for the exclusive use of the Natives and eighty-seven per cent left for the Whites.

In a minute published with the report, Sir William Beaumont wrote: 'The Commission would have liked to frame its recommendations on broad lines. The advantage of large compact areas . . . are so apparent that they need not be enlarged upon . . . But it was found impossible to follow consistently this principle on account of the objections which were raised to the inclusion of European-owned farms within the proposed Native areas. The nature and extent of the proposed Native areas have been largely determined by this objection. A more generous partitioning would have given the Natives less cause for denouncing the Commission's report as unfair to them.'

Yet even as it was, the Beaumont plan created such an outcry among the White landowners that the Government appointed five local committees to revise the Commission's recommendations and make further suggestions. The reports of these local committees reduced the 'released areas' to about fifteen million acres. The suggestions in them were referred to a Select Committee of Parliament which struck a balance between the different plans and recommended that 6,789,544 morgen, or about sixteen million acres, should be earmarked as 'released areas'.

After his ejection from the Botha Government, Hertzog formed the National Party which stated that the basis of its Native policy was 'the dominance of the European population in the spirit of Christian trusteeship with the strictest avoidance of any attempt at race mixture'. The Native, it said, 'must be given the opportunity to develop according to his natural aptitude'.

The Botha Government had to handle some Native trouble as early as 1913. The Free State Provincial Council passed an Ordinance giving municipalities the power to issue passes to Native women—up to that time only Native men had to carry passes. The women refused to obey the law and hundreds of them were charged in the courts and sent to prison. The struggle went on for a long time but in the end the Provincial Council withdrew the Ordinance.

The African National Congress and its newspaper carried on a vigorous campaign on behalf of the women resisters. The Congress sent a deputation to the Acting Prime Minister (F. S. Malan) to protest against the pass laws, which it declared had been passed 'for the purpose of slavery'. Malan denied that that was so and said the laws had been passed for the protection of uncivilized Natives, though he added that he was in favour of granting exemptions to civilized Natives on an increasing scale.

In 1913 there was also further trouble with the Indians. The Supreme Court declared that only Christian marriages were legal, and there were loud protests from the Indian women. The Indian labourers in Natal were also protesting against the £3 poll tax, and strikes broke out. Gandhi led a march of Indians from Natal into the Transvaal and was arrested, as were several White sympathisers with the Indians. The disturbances and the Union Government's way of dealing with them aroused popular indignation in India and the Viceroy made a speech strongly criticising the Union Government. Smuts then agreed to the appointment of a special commission to investigate the position. The commission recommended the abolition of the £3 tax and the restoration of the legal status of Indian married women. The Union Government acted upon these recommendations and also repealed the Indian pass law in the Transvaal.

During the 1914 session of Parliament the Government put through the Riotous Assemblies Act which prohibited the distribution of documents calculated to engender feelings of hostility between Whites and any other sections of the community—the first of numerous enactments on the same lines.

The utterances of the heads of the Allied Powers during and

after the First World War led to a marked change in the outlook of the non-White peoples. In 1919 the first Pan-African Congress sat in Paris and the African National Congress sent delegates to it. The Congress appealed to the League of Nations to formulate an international code to protect the Negroes in Africa and give them greater opportunities for advancement. Another resolution declared that the Native peoples ought to have the right to share in the government of their countries 'as fast as their development permits'.

The delegates from the African National Congress went to Versailles, where the peace treaties were being negotiated. They secured an interview with Lloyd George and recounted the grievances of the Blacks in South Africa, but were unable to obtain any promise of relief. The British Colonial Office told them that the British Government could not interfere in the internal affairs of the Union of South Africa and advised them to return and submit their grievances to the Union Government.

The new spirit among the Natives found expression in an attempt to get rid of the pass laws, the administration of which sent hundreds of thousands of them to prison and aroused a feeling of bitter resentment at the methods adopted by the police.

In 1919 a passive resistance movement was begun under the leadership of the African National Congress. On March 31 several thousand Natives went to the Pass Office in Johannesburg and sent in a deputation to protest against the pass system. The officials on duty could make no promises, and the crowd proceeded to Von Brandis Square and held a meeting at which it was resolved not to carry passes. The passes of all those at the meeting were collected, and pickets went round the town asking the Natives they met to hand over their passes. The police then intervened and numerous Natives were arrested and charged with 'disturbing the public peace'. Rioting broke out and the police charged the crowds.

The White population became alarmed at the attitude of the Natives and there were clashes between White and Black. Meetings called by the African National Congress were broken up by Europeans, some of whom used firearms. Some seven hundred Natives were arrested. Allegations of rough treatment by the police both in the streets and in the cells led to the appointment of a one-man commission to investigate the charges. The Commissioner exonerated the police 'in view of the difficult circumstances', but suggested that the Government should modify the pass laws as it appeared to him that the Natives were determined to resist them.

There was further trouble when the 'night soil boys' in Johannesburg stopped work. There was then no water-borne sewage system in the town, and the Natives operating what were known locally as 'the iron-clads' struck for more pay. The authorities drafted in Native police to carry on the work, but the condition of the town became very unpleasant. The strikers, 152 in number, were arrested and sentenced to two months imprisonment under the Masters and Servants Act. Five Natives (leading members of the African National Congress) were charged with inciting to violence, though in the end the case against them was dropped.

After the end of the First World War the political parties in the Union were chiefly concerned with the growing demands of Afrikaner nationalism and the repercussions of industrial unrest. There was minor legislation affecting the non-Europeans which did not provoke any marked differences of opinion among the Whites.

After Botha's death in 1919 Smuts became Prime Minister. He wished to establish better relations between the Government and the Natives. In 1920 he put through the Native Affairs Act which recognized the desirability of consulting the Bantu in matters affecting them. The Act established the Native Affairs Commission. Its function was to consider all matters relating to the Natives and submit recommendations to the Minister. It was to be 'the friend of the Native people'. It began its work in April 1921 and for many years carried out its duties with marked success.

The need for a segregation policy was again stressed by the Transvaal Local Government Commission of 1922 presided over by Colonel C. F. Stallard a Transvaal member of Parliament well-known for his strong pro-British views. In its report the Commission said: 'The Native should only be allowed to enter urban areas, which are essentially the White man's creation, when he is willing to enter and administer to the needs of the White man, and should depart therefrom when he ceases to minister'. It spoke of the 'peril' of a redundant Black population and advised the creation of municipal Native Affairs departments.

The report led to the passing of the Native Urban Areas Act which gave the local authorities a measure of control over the movements of Natives in the towns. All Natives not employed as servants were required to live in locations, and employers could be called upon to provide suitable accommodation for Natives in their service. As a result of this legislation the municipalities began to embark upon housing schemes for Natives. The Act was amended in later years to provide for the stricter application of the segregation policy.

The Smuts Government had to devote much time and effort to dealing with industrial conflicts. In February, 1920, a large number of Natives working on the gold mines came out on strike. The police cordoned off the properties and the men soon went back to work. The African National Congress called a meeting in support of the strikers and it was broken up by armed European civilians.

Then in 1922 there was a strike of White miners which grew into what was known as the Red Revolt and had to be suppressed by the armed forces of the Government with the use of artillery and bombing aeroplanes.

The upheaval was followed by a long period of depression. There was widespread unemployment among the Europeans in the towns and relief measures had to be organized.

The problem of what was called 'Poor White-ism' also became a national issue. It was estimated that there were between 200,000 and 300,000 Poor Whites (mainly Afrikaners) in the country and that their number was increasing. The Dutch Reformed Church established special irrigation settlements in which impoverished rural families could be provided with small farms the produce from which could be sold in church stores. Hertzog's National Party and the Labour Party began to demand a country-wide effort to employ more White labour. They called for a White South Africa policy.

CHAPTER V

Hertzog Demands Segregation

The launching of Hertzog's National Party to oppose the policy of racial conciliation urged by Botha's South African Party had split the Afrikaners. The schism dominated politics for twenty years and drove even the colour question into the background.

When Hertzog marched into the wilderness in 1912 he seemed to have wrecked his political career. He had only five supporters in the House of Assembly. But after Botha sided with Great Britain in the First World War (in which Hertzog had demanded neutrality) and Smuts became a member of the British War Cabinet, the Hertzogites made converts rapidly. They called for a stronger Afrikaner policy and stumped the backveld denouncing Botha as an 'Engelsman' and Smuts as the 'handy man of the Empire' and the 'valet of Britain'.

Soon the National Party had won so many seats in Parliament that Smuts had to rely upon the votes of the official Opposition, the mainly British Unionist Party, to keep him in office. To save his position Smuts negotiated a merger of his party with the Unionists and became the leader of an enlarged South African Party composed of Afrikaners and Britishers.

Hertzog's National Party then became the official Opposition in Parliament. Hertzog supported the Labour Party in its criticism of Smuts after the 'Red Revolt' and also in its demand for the more general use of White labour in order to entrench the Europeans more securely in South Africa.

Thus the dividing line in politics tended to become economic rather than racial, for both Nationalists and Labourites made their drive at the poorer part of the White community which contained Afrikaners and British. They promised a higher standard of living and less unemployment. There was no mention of the split in

47

Afrikanerdom in their appeal. Yet indirectly it helped the National Party by drawing the poorer Afrikaners away from Smut's South African Party which contained a large number of well-to-do Afrikaners.

The Nationalists and the Labourites also raised the cry that the White race was in danger because it did not play a sufficient part in the everyday work of the country. They found fresh material for their campaign when the report on the 1921 census was published. It was the work of the Director of Census, C. W. Cousins, a well-known civil servant. He made estimates of the probable increase of the different races and arrived at the conclusion that by 1971 there might be in the Union only 3,650,000 Whites and over 19,000,000 Blacks. He penned this warning: 'If the White race is to hold its own in South Africa it will be necessary to secure an immense development of White civilization during the next fifty years, or perhaps only twenty-five years. This comparatively short period may, and in all probability will, decide once and for all the issue upon which speculation has turned—whether the White race is to have any part in the ultimate development of South Africa or whether it is to be entirely crowded out by the aboriginal population.'

This issue drew the Nationalists and the Labourites closer together. The Labour Party programme demanded 'the extension of the field of employment for White persons' and advocated the separation of the Native and White races as far as possible, and the prohibition of intermarriage and cohabitation between Natives and Whites. It also suggested 'the development of suitable industries such as cotton and sugar planting in the Reserves in order to provide for Natives who in pursuance of the White labour policy may be displaced from the areas occupied by Whites'.

When the 1923 session of Parliament opened Hertzog proposed a vote of no-confidence in the Government, and in a debate lasting a week the Nationalists and the Labourites united in denouncing the sins of the Smuts regime. Hertzog and Creswell, the parliamentary leader of the Labour Party, struck up a close friendship, and Tielman Roos, the leader of the Transvaal Nationalists, began to talk openly of a Nationalist-Labour alliance to defeat the Smuts Government. Negotiations between the two parties proceeded smoothly and on April 23, 1923, the Nationalist-Labour Pact came into being.

Events favoured the Pact. A drought depressed the farmers. A world-wide slump caused a falling off in trade. The Government was compelled to retrench and also to increase taxation, and both processes raised up hordes of enemies. It lost still more by-elections. In February 1921 Smuts had a majority of twenty-four in the House of Assembly. By March 1924 his majority had fallen to eight.

In April 1924 there came a vacancy in the Wakkerstroom division in the Transvaal. Smuts set his heart upon stopping the rot. He persuaded the Administrator of the Transvaal, A. G. Robertson, a farmer in the constituency personally popular with both races, to resign his position and fight the seat as the nominee of the South African Party. When heads were counted it was found that the Government's strongest candidate had been defeated by 213 votes by an unknown Nationalist, a cripple from the Boer War. It was the last straw. The next day Smuts, without consulting his Cabinet, went to Parliament and announced that there would be an immediate dissolution and an appeal to the country. The general election was fought with great determination. When the votes were counted it was found that the South African Party had won only 53 seats while the National Party had 63 and Labour 18. Smuts was defeated in Pretoria and three of his Ministers also lost their seats.

The Nationalist-Labour Pact had a majority of twenty-eight in the elected Chamber. Smuts resigned without waiting for Parliament to meet and the Governor-General sent for Hertzog. Twelve years after being ejected from the Union's first Ministry he was asked to form its fourth.

In his history of South Africa, Professor Eric Walker wrote of the result of the 1924 election: 'It was the end of a chapter. Men of British and Afrikaner stock stood shoulder to shoulder in the country and sat together on either side of the House. The old 'racial' lines of division were cut clean across by the economic. The re-alignment of parties was proof that the two sections of the Europeans realized that the issues on which they had hitherto divided were as nothing to the issues raised by their contact with non-Europeans. South Africans were at last fully conscious that they stood face to face with "Black Africa" and "Yellow Asia". Wherefore the new Premier, head of a coalition pledged above all things to the fostering of "White South Africa" addressed himself to a study of the Native Question which had exercised Van Riebeeck in the beginning.'

Hertzog set himself to the task of implementing the White South Africa policy. He took the portfolio of Native Affairs in addition to his task as Prime Minister.

First he tackled the position of the Europeans. A circular was sent out from the Prime Minister's office to all State departments. It laid down as a matter of definite policy that wherever practicable civilized labour should be substituted in all employment by the Government for that which could be classed as uncivilized. Civilized and uncivilized labour were defined in these terms:

> 'Civilized labour is to be considered as the labour rendered by persons whose standard of living conforms to the standard generally recognized as tolerable from the usual European standpoint. Uncivilized labour is to be regarded as the labour rendered by persons whose aim is restricted to the bare requirements of the necessities of life as understood among barbarous and undeveloped peoples.'

The circular insisted that juvenile White labour must be employed wherever possible. It concluded with an injunction that the policy indicated was a serious attempt on the part of the Government to set an example to employers throughout the country and that the Government relied upon every official to do his utmost to promote satisfactory results.

In all departments an effort was made to employ more Whites. The wastage of Indians and Natives on the State railways was made good by engaging Europeans. In June 1924 when the Hertzog Government came into office, there were 5,301 White workers on the railways system. By February 1928 the number had risen to 15,116. In the same period there was a reduction of 9,815 in the number of Indians, Natives and convicts employed on the lines.

The Government tried to protect the White workers in the gold mines. A Commission set up in 1925 reported that the introduction of machinery capable of being worked by experienced Natives threatened the place of the White worker in the entire range of mining operations. It also declared: 'What we have called "colour bar" regulations will go some way towards affecting not only the safety and health generally, but also of counteracting the force of the economic advantages at present enjoyed by the Natives.'

Backed by this report the Government put through an Act

re-establishing the colour bar in mining, which the courts had found to be *ultra vires*.

In 1925 a new taxation system for Natives was introduced. Every male Native who reached the age of eighteen years had to pay a poll tax, known as the general tax, of £1 a year, and in addition the occupier of every hut or dwelling had to pay a local tax of ten shillings per hut per annum. The maximum local tax payable by any Native was £2. Provision was made for the exemption from payment of either or both taxes of indigent Natives not able to work.

The Act created a special fund for the maintenance, extension and improvement of educational facilities for the Bantu. The changes meant that the taxation of the Bantu was taken out of the hands of the Provinces and made a matter for the Union Government. The administration of elementary education for the Natives remained with the Provinces, but the principle was laid down that any development or extension of Bantu education beyond the standard reached in 1921–22 should be financed out of direct taxation paid by the Bantu.

Owing to the activities of the Industrial and Commercial Union—a trade union for Natives which had a large membership—and the Communist Party, the Minister of Justice (Tielman Roos) declared in 1926 that it might be necessary to bring in a Sedition Bill to check the incitement of Natives against the Government. It would in the case if White men however apply only to 'very extreme instances, such as the few hundred Bolsheviks who are inciting the Natives'.

The measure took the form of the Native Administration Act which was passed in 1927. It declared that the Governor-General (really the Cabinet) was the Supreme Chief of all the Natives in Natal, the Transvaal and the Orange Free State and as such possessed all the powers which he had as Supreme Chief in Natal. The powers thus granted were far-reaching. They included the power of immediate arrest and punishment of a Native who defied an order, the detention for three months of any Native who in the opinion of the Supreme Chief might be dangerous to the public peace if left at large, and the exclusion of the jurisdiction of the courts over the acts of the Supreme Chief.

Thus the Government could by proclamation amend or repeal any existing law and make new laws for Natives.

The Act also contained what was called the 'hostility clause'.

This made 'the uttering of any words . . . with intent to promote any feeling of hostility between Natives and Europeans' an offence. The penalty on conviction was imprisonment for a period not exceeding a year, or a fine of £100, or both.

In its enforcement of the White South Africa policy the Hertzog Government also dealt with the Indian question.

In many of the small towns in the Transvaal and Natal a large proportion of the European traders had been driven out of business by Asiatic competition. Municipal authorities had tried to protect the Whites by refusing to grant trading licences to Asiatics and their policy had led to numerous appeals to the courts.

As Minister of the Interior, Dr. D. F. Malan introduced the Areas Reservation and Immigration and Registration Bill which he said was based on the general assumption that the Indians were an alien element in the population and that no solution of the problem would be acceptable unless it resulted in a decrease in their numbers. He pledged the Government to a policy of repatriation.

When the terms of the Bill were published there were strong protests from India and from Great Britain. A deputation from India arrived, and later a deputation from the Union, headed by Malan himself, visited India. After prolonged negotiations there was a conference which resulted in what was called the Cape Town Agreement of January 1927.

The main provisions of the Agreement were that both Governments re-affirmed their recognition of South Africa's right to use all fair means to maintain Western standards of life, and it was also understood that the South African Government could not take steps that were in advance of public opinion. The Union Government agreed to drop the Areas Reservation Bill, a system of voluntary assisted emigration to India was laid down and the Indian Government recognized its obligation to look after such emigrants on their arrival in India. The Union Government on its part agreed that Indians domiciled in the Union who were prepared to conform to Western standards of life should be enabled to do so.

Finally the Cape Town Agreement contained the famous 'Uplift Clause' which read:

'The Union Government firmly believes in and adheres to the principle that it is the duty of every civilized government to devise ways and means and to take all possible steps for the uplifting of every section of their permanent population to the full extent of their capacity and opportunities. The Union Government accepts the view that in the provision of education and other facilities, the considerable number of Indians who will remain part of the permanent population shall not be allowed to lag behind other sections of the people.'

The Union Government also requested India to appoint an Agent in the Union—a proposal which, when made by India in 1922, the Smuts Government had turned down. The first Indian Agent-General in the Union was the Rt. Hon. S. Sastri.

To implement one aspect of the Cape Town Agreement the Immigration and Indian Relief Act of 1928 was passed. It provided financial assistance and free passages for Indians and their families who wished to emigrate. By the end of 1940 over 17,500 Indians had been sent to India, though during the same period over 2,200 wives and children of Indians domiciled in the Union were allowed to enter.

Fortified by enquiries undertaken by various bodies, Hertzog made a sustained effort to place the Native question on a more satisfactory basis. He had taken the portfolio of Native Affairs in order to implement the segregation policy he had expounded when he was Minister of Native Affairs in the first Union Government.

Speaking at Smithfield soon after taking office as Prime Minister he explained that by segregation he meant that the Natives would have their own well-defined areas in which the great mass of them would reside. Those who wished to go out and work for the Whites could do so, for Native labour was indispensable to White civilization; but he wished to prevent a mixture of races that would lead eventually to bastardization. White people must therefore be kept out of the areas in which the Natives lived and *vice versa*. If there was not enough land for the Natives the State must buy more for them, for the matter admitted of no delay as every day made it more complex.

Hertzog rejected the idea that there could be any sharing of government with the Natives. There was an outbreak of violence in one of the locations and in commenting on it he said: 'We are dealing here with the place of the Native, not in a Native territory, but in the land of the White man where the White man shall rule and have the right to live safely and peacefully. Nobody compels the Native to settle in this territory, but if he does so it is demanded from his that he shall respect the White man and obey the laws of the country . . . I would again like to assure the Native that the White man entertains for him the greatest goodwill and the friendliest feelings, and that the White man is determined to carry out faithfully that fatherly care which he has promised to the Native ever since the foundation of the White man's settlement in South Africa . . . I would however warn him at the same time that the White man is just as determined as in the days of the pioneers that the control of the country shall be held by the Europeans under the influence of European civilization and that just as little as the father in his own house would allow a minor to rule the house, would the White man of the Union allow the government of the Union and its people to be held by the Native, or would the Native be given authority within or over the government of the country. I wish to warn the Natives that whoever is so presumptuous as to claim equal authority with the White man will experience the greatest disappointment and failure.'

Hertzog was opposed to the Native franchise in the Cape and said that unless it was amended 'it will spread within forty years to the North, and that would be one of the greatest calamities in our history.'

On the other hand, he desired to keep the Coloured people on the side of the Whites. The Coloured man, he said, 'could not be grouped with the Natives. He had his origin and existence in our midst. He knows no other civilization than that of the White man. However often he falls short of it his outlook is essentially that of the Whites and not of the Natives, and his mother tongue is that of the White man. In his case there can be no talk of segregation.'

To carry out his policy Hertzog drafted four Bills and presented them to Parliament in 1926. One dealt with the Coloured people and the other three with the Natives.

A Bill on Native representation deprived the Natives in the Cape of the franchise they had enjoyed since 1853 but gave them instead the right to elect seven Whites to represent them in the Union House of Assembly and four in the Senate. These representatives were not to be entitled to vote on a matter of confidence unless Native interests were directly concerned.

A second Native Bill set up a Native Council partly nominated and partly elected which would have power to enact Native ordinances under strict control.

A third Native Bill made provision for the acquisition of land by Natives in their own territories in accordance with promises made in 1913.

The fourth Bill confirmed the Coloured vote in the Cape and extended it over the whole of the country. It provided that the Coloured voters outside the Cape would be entitled to return to the Union Parliament one representative of European descent. (The Coloured people condemned the Bill, which never came before Parliament.)

The three Native Bills were sent to a Select Committee in which some sections of them were strongly opposed. The Select Committee reported in 1929, and the Native Franchise Bill was placed before a joint sitting of both Houses and passed by 74 votes to 69: but as a two-thirds majority required 117 votes in favour the Bill was marked as not having been passed.

Hertzog then withdrew his Coloured Voters Bill and in view of the approach of a general election the whole question was dropped.

Smuts's attitude in these discussions was that no solution of the Native question could be secured by forcing measures through Parliament and that a national convention should be called to devise a scheme likely to be acceptable to the majority in both parties and thus able to obtain the two-thirds majority at a joint sitting necessary to place such a measure on the Statute Book.

After the 1914-1918 war there had been widespread movement in many parts of the world to improve the conditions under which non-Europeans lived. In South Africa there were launched societies of Europeans anxious to do more for the welfare of the Natives. In Johannesburg in 1921 there was formed a Joint Council of Europeans and Natives, its aim being to 'establish better race relations through common discussions and co-operative effort'.

The idea was taken up in other parts of the country and before long some thirty Joint Councils had come into existence. It was then felt that there was room for a nation-wide central body to co-ordinate their activities. Thus in May 1929 there was formed the Institute of Race Relations with Dr. C. T. Loram as chairman and J. D. Rheinallt Jones as its adviser. Its object was to 'initiate investigations upon social, economic and other problems with a view to the accumulation of information and the dissemination of knowledge upon matters affecting race relations in South Africa'.

The Institute soon grew into a national body in which European and Native leaders strove to improve race relations. It did not advocate the indiscriminate granting of 'equality' as such, but urged equality of opportunity. It was non-political and non-party and was prepared to criticize any Government in office in order to change unsatisfactory economic and social relations and prevent the drifting apart of Whites and Non-Whites into hostility.

The Institute and the Joint Councils convened a national conference on Hertzog's Native Bills and issued a pamphlet asking whether it was wise to abolish the Native franchise in the Cape. It argued that it would be better from a European point of view to allow individual Natives to exercise the vote rather than that a separate organization of solidly race-conscious Natives should be forced into being.

In 1928 there was Native trouble in Natal. All over South Africa it was a penal offence for a Native to possess spirits or wine and for a European to supply them to Blacks. In the towns, however, Bantu women brewed Native beer for sale and though the practice was illegal it was widespread.

A number of municipalities in Natal, acting under a new provincial law, decided to brew Native beer themselves and open canteens in which it could be sold to Natives. The Bantu women then called for a boycott of the canteens and picketed them. The police intervened and there was fighting between the women and the constables. The trouble grew when bands of Whites raided the offices of the Industrial and Commercial Union in Durban and rioting resulted in which six Natives and two Europeans were killed. The judge who conducted a commission of inquiry into the trouble reported that had irresponsible Whites not beleaguered the I.C.U. offices there would have been no conflict between the police and the mob.

The canteen boycott went on for some months. It was said too that the Natives in Durban were not paying their taxes and armed police paraded the town and made a house-to-house search for defaulters. Large crowds of Natives assembled in the streets and the police dispersed them with tear-gas bombs. The next day hundreds of Natives paid their taxes. Tear gas was seen to be a useful weapon and in succeeding years it was employed more frequently.

Meanwhile the 1929 general election came round. Hertzog's National Party launched its appeal to the electorate on the White South Africa cry.

It so happened that General Smuts made a speech at Ermelo in which he was reported to have said: 'The day will surely come when we shall not think of the Limpopo only but when the British States in Africa will all become members of a great African dominion stretching unbroken throughout Africa . . . We shall be a friend of our fellow African States and shall look for a united British Africa. That is the cardinal point in my policy. When the South African Party comes into power again it will do its best to foster that spirit of co-operation and brotherliness which will in the end lead to this great African federation of States. The term South Africa will surely be dropped from our national vocabulary and there will be a united British South Africa which will find the solution of our pressing problems an easy matter.'

Upon the publication of the report of this speech, Hertzog, Tielman Roos and Dr. D. F. Malan (the leader of the Cape National Party) issued a manifesto denouncing Smuts as 'a man who puts himself forward as the apostle of a Black Kafir State of which South Africa is to form so subordinate a constituent part that she will know her name no more', and who preaches the doctrine of "equal political rights for all—Kafirs and White men everywhere—on an equal footing".'

What was at stake, declared the manifesto, was the continued existence or the downfall of the White man and his civilization in South Africa. It embraced the question whether the people of South Africa should passively stand by and watch South Africa wiped off the map, as General Smuts desired, in order to be dissolved into a huge Kafir State stretching from the Cape to the Sudan.

The manifesto went on to say that the issue raised was greater than party interests or than the differences between one White race and the other. 'It is evident that General Smuts is here bidding farewell to South Africa as a White man's country. The cardinal point in his policy is that South Africa shall form part of a country embracing the Kafir territories in the north up to the Sudan.'

On the day the manifesto was published, Smuts, in the House of Assembly, ridiculed the attack upon him and denied that his speech could possibly bear the construction the signatories had placed upon it. The South African Party denounced the manifesto as 'the most scandalous document ever issued in Union politics'.

The manifesto probably had considerable influence in the rural districts. From farm to farm and from dorp to dorp the cry went up that Smuts wanted to give the vote to Kafirs. Tens of thousands of cards were distributed bearing the appeal: 'Voters vote National-ist and save our children from the Black policy of the South African Party.'

At the polls the National Party won 78 seats and the South African Party 61. The Labour Party secured only 8 seats, as against 18 in 1924. The Pact Government's majority in the House of Assembly fell from 28 to 19. Hertzog was, however, able to dissolve the Senate in which his party had been in a minority and obtain a new one in which he could rely upon a majority.

After the election Tielman Roos retired from politics and was appointed an Appeal Court judge. Ostensibly he stepped down owing to ill health. It was known however that he disagreed with Hertzog upon several points, more particularly on the idea of extending the Coloured vote all over the Union.

Despite disagreement behind the scenes, the Pact Government pushed on with its measures. The dominance of the White electorate was increased in 1930 when the franchise was conferred upon White women and not upon Coloured women. In 1931 all European males over the age of twenty-one were given the vote— a change which increased the number of electors of Dutch descent.

Mr. Oswald Pirow, a Pretoria barrister, took Tielman Roos's place as Minister of Justice. In 1930 he put through Parliament an amendment to the Riotous Assemblies Act which gave the Minister increased power. Under it the Minister was not required to wait for a conviction before acting. Whenever he was satisfied that any person in any area was promoting feelings of hostility between Europeans and Non-Europeans he could deliver a note to him prohibiting him from being in any defined area. If the per-son did not comply with the terms of the order he could be punished with imprisonment and could still be removed from the area in which he had been prohibited to be.

The new power was challenged in the courts and the case came before Mr. Justice Stratford, who remarked that the provisions of the Act constituted a measure of 'preventive justice'. They were not directed towards punishment for offences committed but 'towards restraining a man from committing a crime he may commit but has not yet committed, or doing some act injurious to members of the community which he may do but has not yet done.'

The Judge added that there was no doubt that the Act made a serious inroad upon the ordinary liberty of the subject; but Parliament had conferred upon the Minister the power to act promptly when he thought certain conditions existed. He continued: 'Bearing in mind the kind of situation and the nature of the apprehended danger which the legislature clearly has in contemplation, it will readily be seen that if the Minister's discretion is hampered by the obligation to submit his decision to the approval of a court of law the delay involved would defeat the whole object of the particular provision we are discussing . . . Once we are satisfied on the construction of the Act, that it gives to the Minister an unfettered discretion, it is no function of a court of law to curtail its scope in the least degree . . . Parliament may make any encroachment it chooses upon the life, liberty or property of any individual subject to its sway, and it is the function of the courts of law to enforce its will".

The new law was applied, and numerous individuals were ordered to leave specified areas and remain away for considerable periods. All African National Congress meetings in the country districts of the Western Province of the Cape were prohibited under the Act.

The Communist Party launched a pass-burning movement but with very little success, though many of its members were charged and convicted. The introduction of the 'pick-up van' by the police led to disorders in Johannesburg and along the Rand.

Probably the Pact Government could have carried on for its full term of five years, for Hertzog, despite intrigues within his party, commanded the support of the mass of the Afrikaners. The test was not made. Unexpected events beyond the borders of the Union led to a new alignment of parties.

Great Britain went off the gold standard on September 21, 1931, and Hertzog decided that as the Union was a gold-producing country it ought not to follow suit. The attempt to remain on gold failed, and on December 28, 1932, the Union was forced off gold and Hertzog and Smuts formed a coalition government to see the country through the crisis.

The Coalition went to the country in May 1933 and obtained an enormous majority. The two big parties under Hertzog and Smuts had retained their separate identity, but finally a plan for fusion was adopted and the United Party came into being and Hertzog carried on as Prime Minister with Smuts as Deputy Prime Minister.

The Native policy of the United Party was thus defined: 'An earnest endeavour will be made to arrive at a satisfactory solution of the Native question along lines which, without depriving the

Native of his right of development, will recognize as paramount the essentials of European civilization. It is recognized that a solution of the political aspect of this question on the basis of separate representation of Europeans and Natives, or otherwise, being fundamental in character and not having hitherto been a matter of party division, should as far as possible be sought through agreement and should be left to the free exercise of the discretion of the individual members representing the party in Parliament.'

Dr. Malan and the Cape National Party refused to agree to the fusion plan and formed the Purified National Party, which became the official Opposition and carried on a fierce campaign against the Hertzog-Smuts Government.

Having now a huge majority in both Houses of Parliament, Hertzog set himself to the task of obtaining legislative sanction for the segregation policy he had first propounded nearly a quarter of a century earlier.

Support for his ideas was provided in the findings of the Native Economic Commission which had been appointed in June 1930, and reported early in 1932. The commission was presided over by Dr. J. E. Holloway, who in later years became Secretary of the Treasury and represented the Union both in America and the United Kingdom.

The Commission reported that the drift of raw Natives into the towns resulted in the labour market being in a chronic state of chaos. No regular class of urban labour could develop because Natives who remained permanently in the towns were always subjected to the disturbing influence on wage rates of a large supply of unskilled labour, which also incidentally created a big slum population.

'It is essential,' declared the Commission, 'that no time shall be lost both in developing the Reserves and in reducing the present pressure on land by making available more areas for Native occupation. While present conditions last the flow to the towns will continue, the pressure on the urbanized Native will increase, and the problem of Native wages in towns will become worse. State policy should be directed to reducing the pressure in the interests of the welfare of a class of Natives who have made considerable progress in civilization and with whose aspirations for conditions in which better living is possible one cannot but have the fullest sympathy.'

The Commission stressed this point very strongly. It insisted that the cure for most of South Africa's ills 'lies in a wise courageous forward policy of development of the Reserves.' A large portion of the Reserves possessed agricultural potentialities which were not exceeded elsewhere in the Union. It would be wise to develop the wealth-producing capacity of these excellent areas and thus secure a larger amount to go round, rather than to allow a continuance of the present struggle between Black and White for a larger share of the wealth being produced from the developed areas.

Under the heading 'Segregation' the Commission reported:

'The word "segregation" is frequently used in connection with Native questions. A great deal of confusion is caused by its employment in different senses, and it will therefore be advantageous to examine here some of them in so far as they affect the social and economic condition of the Natives. Full economic segregation would mean that the Europeans and the Natives would be put into separate areas and that they would not be allowed to work for each other. Nobody advocated this. It would be impossible, and uneconomical even if possible because it would deprive the European of the labour of the Native and the latter of the guidance, management and largely, too, of the capital of the European. What is generally advocated under the heading segregation may be termed partial economic segregation. Most people favour some form of this; but there is a great divergence of opinion as to the degree of segregation which it would involve. Views have been expressed which would mean that the Natives should live in a part of the country set aside for them, and that individuals should be admitted into the European area on temporary permit to work; that they should not however make their homes in the European area, and those who have made their homes should be gradually transferred to the Native area.

'Your Commissioners cannot give any support to this view. Besides being impracticable it would be unfair to Natives who have already become permanent town-dwellers, or dwellers on European farms. Moreover it would mean that Native labour in the European area would always be casual labour, and if this were to continue there would be great difficulty in the way of increasing its efficiency. This would be a very bad outlook for European industry since the maintenance of the present low rate of efficiency of Native labour must as long as it lasts continue to be a serious drawback in the attainment of higher efficiency in industry as a whole.

'There is however,' continued the Commissioners, 'a form of partial segregation which lies at the basis of your Commission's report. This consists in developing the Native areas sufficiently to make greater provision for the needs of the Natives resident therein. The effect of this will be that the classes of urban and rural labour will tend to crystalize to an extent which will enable greater efficiency to be achieved by both. The urban labourer will then be in a position that he can emerge from the present unfair competition of the casual rural labourer. The towns would be less inundated by the latter, because the competition of the more efficient regular town-dwellers would make the conditions less attractive to them. A considerable number of Natives from the Reserves would still have to come out from time to time to work. They would however flow into channels where casual labour is regularly required. Mining would offer scope as at present for a large proportion of these labourers; and as the development of the Reserves would interest the Natives in better agriculture it might be expected that there would grow up a class of more or less specialized land-workers from which there would be available a surplus of labour naturally gravitating to casual work on European farms as it was required there. The effect should therefore be to create a more economical distribution of the labour forces than obtain now.'

The members of the Native Economic Commission were impressed by the undeveloped condition of the Reserves, which they found included some of the richest land in the Union. They said that a comparison of a map of South Africa distinguishing the Native areas, with a rainfall chart, showed that the Natives a as whole have no reason to complain of the moisture condition of their lands judged by the general rainfall distribution of the country.

The Commission sounded one warning note. It said: 'The growth of a Native nationalism, or race consciousness, is a factor which is not yet generally recognized by the Europeans of the Union, but it is one which must be kept clearly in view when questions affecting the Natives' social and economic positions are being considered. It cannot safely be ignored or suppressed.'

At that time some of the leaders of the Natives were not opposed to the principle of separation provided that certain conditions were laid down. In 1931 six of them drew up a statement for circulation among members of Parliament. It contained the following:

'The principle of creating Reserves in which Natives will be enabled to attain a high standard of economic production under a system of local self-government will certainly receive the support of every intelligent Native leader. But those Reserves must fulfil the following conditions:

'(a) In each Province of the Union there should be a large compact Native area like the Transkei, because without such a Reserve Natives cannot develop a real national life, i.e. they cannot develop a becoming race-consciousness.

'(b) In each of the Reserves so created there should be a council to deal with local matters: this council to have more legislative powers and functions than the Transkeian Bunga. Members of the council to be elected by the people.

'(c) In these Reserves the civil service to be open to competent Natives.

'(d) The Reserves should be opened for occupation by any member of the Bantu race.

'(e) Fullest facilities for trading by Natives in the Reserves should be allowed.'

The statement also suggested that there should be a Union Native Council whose members should be elected from the members of similar provincial councils. This Council would deal with all matters affecting the Native people as a whole and would advise the Government on legislation dealing with Natives.

It will be remembered that Hertzog's four Bills dealing with non-Europeans had been referred to a Select Committee of Parliament. A large number of people representing all races and shades of political opinion gave evidence before it. The Committee did not report until 1935, after the fusion of the two big parties. It did not deal with the claims of the Coloured people, and it reduced Hertzog's three Native Bills to two—the Representation of Natives Bill and the Native Trust and Land Bill.

The Representation of Natives Bill transferred the Native voters in the Cape to a special electoral roll and gave them the right to elect three Europeans to the House of Assembly. The Natives in the rest of the Union could, through electoral colleges, choose four Europeans to represent them in the Senate. The measure also provided for the establishment of a Natives Representative Council to report on matters affecting the Natives. It was an advisory body and the Government explained that it was hoped that the Council would give the leaders of the Natives a training ground for the procedure of government and lead to a better understanding between the White and Black races.

In Parliament there was some objection to the Land Bill. The Purified Nationalists criticized it on the ground that there should have been more enquiry before so much land was ear-marked for Natives while many Whites could not obtain farms. The Nationalists however did not vote against the Bill. Indeed Dr. Malan admitted that the Bill 'went in the right direction'. He said that to give land, and sufficient land, to the Natives 'is part of the segregation policy. We cannot get away from that and there is no one who will fairly be able to take up the attitude that we ought to do nothing to make provision for that end.'

Hertzog's Bills however were not acceptable to the Natives. An All-African National Convention was held at Bloemfontein on December 18, 1935, attended by four hundred delegates from all parts of the Union. It passed resolutions condemning the Government's measures. One declared that the proposals for the establishment of a Natives Representative Council were no substitute for the Cape Native franchise. Another denounced the Trust and Land Bill on the ground that it gave a 'gross inadequacy' of land for the Natives and failed to take into account the needs of an increasing Native population. It declared that 'the fact that this aim is ignored can only be interpreted by the African people as an attempt to force them into a position of economic dependency'.

A member of the Cabinet (J. H. Hofmeyr) had voted against the abolition of the Native vote in the Cape and many Europeans agreed with him. They summoned a 'National Conference on the Native Bills' in Cape Town and published a pamphlet dealing with the issue. Arguing that the measure was unwise, the pamphlet proceeded: 'If it be accepted that the Natives must be given some political power it is surely better from the European point of view that this should come by allowing individual Natives to exercise the vote as and when they reach a certain level of civilization than that a separate organization of solidly race-conscious Natives should be forced into being. The hard-headed European would doubtless take account of the possibility that on a common roll the White vote might some day be "swamped" by the Black vote. That is of course proper matter for consideration, but it must be treated soberly and without panic . . . Any system which makes for a higher standard of living tends towards a lower birth rate . . . The method of raising the required qualification to prevent such "swamping" has Cape precedent in its favour and could be used again if required. The figures show beyond question that even on an admittedly low qualification basis the idea of "swamping" is a mere bogey. The Native vote in the Cape amounts to approximately one per cent of the whole Union electorate. It would be simplicity itself to control the number of Native voters by relating the franchise to the attainment of a recognized school standard with or without an income or property qualification.'

In 1937 the Government passed the Industrial Conciliation Act which excluded Natives from the definition of 'employees' and thus from membership of trade unions recognized under the Act. All strikes by Native workers in trade unions not so recognized, or by groups of Natives, were therefore illegal. It was claimed that Native wages in industry were protected by the Wage Act of 1927, or by industrial agreements relating to the trades or industries concerned.

In 1939 the Government put through the Transvaal Land and Trading Act which laid down that an Asiatic must apply for a licence to carry on a business or trade or to remove his business to other premises. A permit had also to be obtained before land or premises not occupied by an Asiatic on April 30, 1939, could be let or occupied by an Asiatic. This measure evoked bitter opposition not only from the Transvaal Indians but from India. Mahatma Gandhi sent a message of protest to South Africa, and Mr. Jinnah, the president of the All-India Moslem League, also condemned the measure. J. H. Hofmeyr and several members of the United Party criticized the Bill on the ground of its discriminatory character and eventually Hofmeyr and Leslie Blackwell (a front-bencher on the Government side in Parliament) resigned from the United Party caucus.

Hertzog expounded his policy for the Coloureds (as distinct from the Bantu) in a statement made in Parliament on March 23, 1939. (In later years however his ideas were rejected by the National Party to which he returned.) His statement contained the following points:

'*Political Status.* The Coloured people are not to be deprived of their existing political rights, and the Government will resist any proposals to change their franchise in a manner that would diminish those rights.

'*Economic Status.* Coloured people shall not by reason of race or colour be debarred from engaging in any form of industrial occupation or employment, but the Government will endeavour to ensure that the working conditions of employment accord with the social policy set out hereunder.

'*Social Status.* There is no desire on the part of either the White or the Coloured people that there shall be social intercourse between them, and social separation is accepted by both as the definite and settled policy of the country. Wherever social or economic conditions conflicting with this policy of social separation are found to exist the Government will do its best to remedy such conditions; but it will always try to do so in a manner that will avoid causing ill-feeling or a sense of grievance and will involve no greater discrimination than the necessities of the case require. The most effective step in this direction is the provision of adequate housing accommodation so that the White and Coloured need not crowd together under slum conditions where it is difficult for the inhabitants to remain socially apart. This step has already been taken on a very large scale and with universal approval. The Government intends to go forward with this policy. Legislation will however be necessary to carry it out. Local authorities are at present not equipped with proper powers to provide for the estab-lishment of separate European and Non-European townships in the future. The Government looks forward to the time when most of the Coloured community will be living happily and contentedly in their own villages, townships or suburbs. It will then be possible to make them responsible for running their own affairs and services as far as practicable. Substantial outlets will thus be found for educated Coloureds among their own community and the friction that now arises will be avoided. In industry the policy of separating Europeans and Non-Europeans, wherever conditions are such that but for that separation there may be social intermingling, is already in force and is being carried out with very willing co-operation on the part of the great bulk of both the employers and the employed concerned. The Government will give effect to this policy in its administration and also, if this course is at any time found necessary, by legislative measures.'

Then once more events overseas brought about a change in the politico-party kaleidoscope in South Africa.

On September 3, 1939, Great Britain entered the Second World War. Hertzog summoned a Cabinet meeting at which he proposed that the Union should remain neutral. Smuts opposed him and had a majority of one on his side. Hertzog then went to

Parliament and introduced a resolution in favour of neutrality. Smuts moved an amendment in favour of entering the war on the side of Great Britain and it was carried by eighty votes to sixty-three.

Hertzog resigned and asked the Governor-General (Sir Patrick Duncan) to dissolve Parliament and submit the issue to the country at a general election. Duncan declined on the ground that Smuts commanded a sufficient majority in Parliament to carry on a government. He sent for Smuts and asked him to form an Administration. Smuts succeeded in doing so backed by members of the United Party, the Dominion Party and the Labour Party.

The African National Congress held a meeting in Durban and adopted a resolution declaring that the decision to fight on the side of Great Britain was correct, but adding that the time had arrived for the Government 'to consider the expediency of admitting Africans and other Non-Europeans into full citizenship of the Union with all the rights, privileges, duties and responsibilities appertaining to that citizenship; and that the territorial integrity of the country could be effectively defended only if all sections of the population were included in the defence system on equal terms.'

After the Smuts Government had been formed, Hertzog and his supporters crossed the floor to the Opposition side of the House and joined Malan's Purified National Party. The official Opposition was then called the Herenigde (Re-united) National Party. Soon however Hertzog's leadership was rejected and he resigned from Parliament and Malan became the unchallenged leader of the Nationalists.

The war made the Union a divided and unhappy country. Many of the Nationalists believed that the Germans would win, neo-Nazi groups were formed and there was a certain amount of sabotage. The Government won the war-time general election of 1943 and had a majority of sixty-four in the elected Chamber.

During the war no fresh Native legislation of importance was placed before Parliament. Smuts wished however to establish better relations with the Non-Whites. In 1944 he issued an instruction to all Government departments that official letters to Coloured persons should be addressed in the same way as to Whites, 'Sir' or 'Madam', and that the envelopes should be addressed 'Mr.' or 'Mrs.'. The depth of feeling on the colour question in South Africa was shown when even this small concession provoked loud protests. A number of officials were dismissed for disobeying the instruction, or resigned their appointment rather than carry it out.

Smuts's effort to conciliate the Non-Europeans met with little response. The rough draft of the Charter of the United Nations, drawn up at Moscow, had been eagerly welcomed by them and they became more militant in their demands for reforms.

Towards the end of 1943 the African National Congress declared that it had three aims—(1) To protect and advance the interests of the African people in all matters affecting them; (2) To attain the freedom of the African people from all discriminatory laws whatever; (3) To strive and work for the unity and co-operation of all African peoples in every possible way.

The Congress denounced the Pass Laws as 'Enemy Number One' and made preparations for the holding of a national anti-pass conference. It was held in Johannesburg in May 1944 and lasted two days. Five hundred and forty delegates claimed to represent over six hundred thousand people. The conference passed a resolution declaring that the Pass Laws held the African people in conditions of abject poverty and subjection and were the cause of sharp racial friction between the peoples of South Africa.

A petition against the Pass Laws was drafted to which it was hoped to obtain a million signatures. The effort was not a marked success and it was not until June 1945 that the petition was taken to Cape Town for presentation to Parliament. The Acting Prime Minister refused to see a deputation, and a mass meeting on the Grand Parade protested against his 'undemocratic refusal to meet the anti-pass deputation representing some million Africans'. A procession was then formed to take the petition to Parliament buildings and there were clashes with the police who finally dispersed the crowd. The leaders of the demonstration were arrested and fined for leading an unlawful procession.

The Congress leaders had been strengthened in their attitude by the pronouncements of the Fifth Pan-African Congress which met in England in 1945 and adopted a more aggressive tone than its predecessors had done. It issued a declaration to the world, which said: 'We are determined to be free. We want education. We want the right to earn a decent living; the right to express our thoughts and emotions, to adopt and create forms of beauty. We demand for Black Africa autonomy and independence so far and no further than it is possible in this one world for groups and peoples to rule themselves subject to inevitable world unity and federation.'

The concluding sentence in the declaration was: 'We shall fight in every way we can for freedom, democracy and our social betterment.'

The delegates to the Fifth Pan-African Congress discussed the passive resistance movement successfully launched by Mahatma Gandhi in India and endorsed it as the only effective way of persuading alien rulers to respect the rights of weak and unarmed subject races. In one of its resolutions the Congress called upon all farmers and workers in the Colonies to organize, and told them: 'Your weapons—the strike and the boycott—are invincible.'

The new spirit revealed at the Pan-African Congress influenced the delegates to the annual conference of the African National Congress held in December 1945. A Bill of Rights was drafted and adopted. It began: 'We the African people in the Union of South Africa urgently demand the granting of full citizenship rights such as are enjoyed by all Europeans in South Africa.'

The Bill of Rights called for the abolition of discrimination based on race, the prohibition of police raids on citizens in their homes, and the right to own land and property without any restrictions. It demanded equal pay for equal work, the removal of the colour bar in industry and the right of the African worker to collective bargaining. It asked for free and compulsory education and the abandonment of the theory that 'there is need for a special type of education for Africans as such'. Africans, it declared, must be given the type of education which would enable them 'to meet on equal terms with other people the conditions of the modern world'.

The final clause of the Bill of Rights read: 'In short we demand the repeal of any and all laws, as well as the abandonment of any policy and all practices that discriminate against the African in any way whatsoever on the basis of race, creed or colour in the Union of South Africa'.

In this mood the Natives Representative Council met on August 15, 1946, under the chairmanship of Dr. Moroka and passed a resolution condemning the 'reactionary nature of the Union's Native policy of segregation in all its different aspects', deploring the adoption by the Smuts Government of 'the policy of Fascism', and calling upon the Government to repeal all discriminatory legislation forthwith.

On November 20, 1946, the Acting Prime Minister, Mr. J. H. Hofmeyr, who was well-known for his liberal views, met the members of the Natives Representative Council and told them it was impossible to accede to their request for the immediate abolition of all discriminatory laws.

The Council then drew up a memorandum stating that their resolution of August 15 was a 'challenge' to the Government to show how far it would be prepared to adjust its Native policy to the changed circumstances of the Native population. On November 16 Mr. Hofmeyr reiterated the decision of the Government that it was impossible to comply with the request to repeal all discriminatory laws. To this refusal the Council replied by adjourning indefinitely.

In announcing its decision to adjourn *sine die*, Dr. Moroka said: 'We shall never be satisfied until the Africans are in a position themselves to help make the laws of the country. We shall continue to fight until the Africans sit next to the Europeans, the Indians and the Coloureds in the legislative assemblies of the land. The Government may repeal all the Pass Laws, it may repeal all the discriminatory legislation and make the greatest concessions, but the Africans will not be satisfied with that. We ourselves want to help rule the country by means of direct representation.'

Six months later Smuts himself met the leading members of the Natives Representative Council and offered to extend the scope of the Council and even to grant it certain limited powers. The majority of the Council rejected his offer on the ground that the proposed concessions did not go to the root of the dispute between the Council and the Government. The Council called for 'a re-orientation of the whole of Native policy and not a mere tinkering with its existing framework. . . . Our present Native policy is not calculated to integrate the African people into the general life of the country. On the contrary it is based on the principle of permanent separation, which engenders a spirit of hostility and racial bitterness between Black and White instead of a spirit of mutual co-operation in the interests of both sections of the country as a whole.'

The Second World War led to an upsurge of African nationalism in many parts of the continent. In the Union it also gave a fresh impetus to Afrikaner nationalism. The seeds of the revival had been sown in 1938 during the centenary celebration of the Great Trek.

An organization called the Ossewa Brandwag (The Path of the Ox) was formed to entrench Afrikaans ideals and culture, and soon it boasted of having over 300,000 members. The Broerderbond, a secret society pledged to place Afrikaners in all important positions in the State, strove to undermine the position of the Smuts Government.

In Parliament the members of Malan's National Party kept up a constant attack upon everything appertaining to England. They accused the Smuts Government of sacrificing South Africa on the altar of British Imperialism, and declared that the only way to safeguard the independence of the country was to adopt a republican form of government. They played upon racial feeling, and many members of the Smuts party moved over to their side, though the 1943 general election did not reflect the change because a large number of Afrikaners had been temporarily disfranchised under the war-time regulations. Like the Botha Government in the 1914-18 war, the Smuts Government emerged on the winning side in the Second World War, but at a cost that was not realized at the moment.

CHAPTER VI

Malan Proclaims Apartheid

Another general election was due in the Union in 1948. Dr. Malan admitted that the country had been against him on the war issue, and that the support his party had given the Germans in the struggle had been ill-advised. He decided to appeal to the electorate on a new issue. Like Hertzog in 1924, he went to the country on the White South Africa cry.

Several considerations influenced his decision. In the first place the Union's 1946 census figures were being published. They showed that the preponderance of the Non-European section of the population was increasing. It was revealed that the Whites in the Union numbered 2,372,690 while the Non-Whites numbered 9,045,659. Since 1910 the White population had increased by little more than a million, whereas the Non-White population had expanded by nearly four-and-a-half millions. In 1910 the Whites had formed 21.4 per cent of the total population. In 1946 they formed only 20.8 per cent of it.

In the second place the small cloud of Bantu nationalism that had appeared on the horizon after the First World War was rapidly becoming bigger, and the Non-European organizations were growing more vocal and aggressive in demanding concessions. They were encouraged by the fact that in 1946 Great Britain had enabled the Gold Coast to become the first colony in tropical Africa to have a Native majority in its Legislative Council, a step which a great many South Africans viewed with dislike. Moreover the Communists were increasing their activities among the African races generally, and were beginning to make propaganda in the Union itself. Many Europeans in South Africa felt that their supremacy was being threatened, and that steps ought to be taken to defend it.

With this background for an appeal to the electorate Malan proclaimed a stronger colour policy, which he called Apartheid (pronounced apart-hate).

Curiously enough he employed a word that had only just begun to be used by the Afrikaners to describe their colour policy. In 1913 Hertzog had called his policy segregation. Smuts, who had very much the same ideas, preferred to speak of separation. For more than thirty years the Union's colour policy was always described either as separation or segregation. When the Transvaal National Party published its programme of principles in 1944 it did not use the word Apartheid. In 1947 however Malan appointed a commision to draw up a Native policy for the National Party. In its report this commission used the word Apartheid more than forty times. Yet an Afrikaans dictionary printed in 1949 did not contain the word.

But when Malan outlined the National Party's programme for the 1948 election he described its Native policy as Apartheid. He spoke at Paarl on April 20, 1948, and declared that the approaching election would be the most important and decisive in the whole of South Africa's political history. There was a question which overshadowed all others and must be regarded before all others by the people who were now going to determine, perhaps for all time, their destiny. That question was 'Whither South Africa?'.

'Will,' Malan went on, 'the European race in the future be able to maintain its rule, its purity and its civilization, or will it float along until it vanishes for ever, without honour, in the Black sea of South Africa's Non-European population? If it can, and wants, to save itself then can it, and does it, want to do so without oppression and in consideration of the Non-Europeans' natural right to a proper living and their right to their own development in accordance with their own requirements and capabilities? Will the ever-encroaching and all-destroying Communist cancer be checked, or will it be further allowed to undermine our freedom, our religion, our own South African nationhood and our European existence, our honourable traditions and our racial and civil peace? Will South Africa shake off those exaggerated foreign complexes of which the present Government is possessed and eventually pay attention to the interests and requirements, and not least to the legitimate grievances, of large sections of our people?'.

'As a result of foreign influences,' he went on, 'the demand for the removal of all colour bars and segregation measures is being pressed more and more continuously and vehemently; and all this means nothing less than that the White race will lose its ruling position and that South Africa will sooner or later have to take its place among the half-caste nations of the world'.

The National Party policy, asserted Malan, was based upon 'the two fundamental principles of separation and trusteeship'.

'As the words themselves indicate,' he said, 'this means in no way the oppression of the Non-Europeans but the elimination of racial friction through the acknowledgment of their right of existence, their freedom of development, coupled with the cultivation among them of a spirit of self-respect and self-reliance and the provision to them of the necessary help, but everything in their own sphere and under the sovereignty and leadership of the Europeans. Apartheid must as far as possible also be applied and maintained between the three sections of the Non-Europeans —Coloured, Native and Indian. The party regards the solution of the colour question on this basis as absolutely necessary. At the same time it regards it as especially desirable that this should be achieved if possible on a non-party basis.'

After explaining that the Apartheid plan would necessitate a general registration of Europeans and Non-Europeans alike, Malan said that the main points of the Apartheid policy in respect of the Non-European groups were as follows:

THE NATIVES

'(1) The Native Reserves must be retained and made suitable for carrying a larger population by protecting the soil against erosion and over-cropping and by teaching the Native to make the best use of his soil by applying better agricultural methods. Possible additions must only take place in judicious fashion and after thorough investigation.

'(2) In urban areas inside the European areas Natives must be domiciled in their own residential areas with proper attention to good housing and other healthy accommodation conditions. Only Natives who have been assured of work will be admitted, and the detribalized ones among them will at all times receive preference. Newcomers from the Native areas or from the European platteland must be regarded as temporary workers and those in excess must be repatriated.

'(3) In view of their possession of their own national home in the Reserves, Natives in the European areas can make no claim to political rights. The present representation of Natives in Parliament and in the Cape Provincial Council must therefore be abolished. Representation in the Senate must however continue by the election of three European Senators by different Native councils and further through three others nominated by the Government because of their particular knowledge of Native affairs, as is now the case. These representatives must form a standing and permanent committee on Native Affairs. They must however have no vote on questions of confidence, or on the declaration of war or on measures affecting the political rights of non-Europeans. The present existing Native Affairs Commission must give way to a more effective commission of experts.

'(4) The present existing Native Advisory Council must be abolished and in its place a system of self-government on the first-rate and well-tried example of the Transkei Bunga called into being—a system which will keep proper account of the natural groupings among the Natives themselves based on the territorial, historical, racial and linguistic differences between them. This will give to the Natives that opportunity of living out their own aspirations which under the present system are being withheld from them and which in their dissatisfaction makes them willing prey of the Communist agitator.

'(5) For higher education separate provision must be made for Natives and their admission to European institutions together with European students must end.

'(6) Administratively all Native interests including education must rest with the department of Native Affairs and the necessary sub-departments.'

THE COLOURED PEOPLE

'(1) The party bases its policy on the fact that the Coloured people form their own separate group between on the one side the Europeans, with whom they share the same language and cultural interests, and on the other side the Natives, from whom they differ in race, language and standard of civilization and above whom they must hold a privileged position in the European areas.

'(2) As against the Europeans the principle of Apartheid must be applied in respect of residential areas, which can only be brought about gradually, and in public transport, recreational areas and as far as possible also in work places. Further in urban areas, as well as in the platteland, provision must be made with Government support for better housing for

Coloured people, special attention being paid to the require ments of the more civilized ones among them, but in any case separately and at a distance from Native locations

'(3) In territories where the Coloured population is largely resident, their interests, particularly in regard to the provision of employment, must be protected against those of Natives flowing in.

'(4) In Coloured residential areas Coloured people must as far as possible be appointed for public positions, and preference must be given to them in the granting of business licences.

'(5) In the provision of educational facilities for Coloured people special account must be taken of their prospects in the service of their own racial group, as well as in connection with the provision of employment in general. Technical education must be provided for them in accordance with their requirements and they must have their own separate university institutions.

'(6) A State department for specially furthering the interests of Coloured people must be called into being in which Coloured people will also serve as civil servants. In this connection a Coloured Advisory Council must also exist, the members of which, apart from a few Government nominees, must be elected by qualified Coloured voters themselves and on the basis of constituencies. The present Coloured Advisory Council, nominated by the Government and dependent on it, must disappear.

'(7) In place of their vote as at present exercised—which makes them the playball of the political parties—special representation must be given to the Coloured people in Parliament through a Senator nominated by the Government because of his special knowledge of Coloured affairs, three members of Parliament chosen by the Coloured Advisory Council, and three members of the Cape Provincial Council chosen on the same basis as those in Parliament. The representatives must be Europeans.'

THE INDIANS

'(1) The party will strive to repatriate or remove elsewhere as many Indians as possible with the co-operation of India and other countries.

'(2) The present ban on Indian immigration, interprovincial movement and penetration must remain and be more stringently maintained.

'(3) The Indian must not be allowed to reside among other racial groups.

'(4) Trading licences to Indians outside their own residential areas must be reduced.

'(5) Family allowances to Indians must be abolished.'

Malan promised that severe measures would be taken against Communist propaganda and infiltration in every form and that the public service would be purged of all Communist influences.

The Nationalists insisted that the Apartheid policy was a long-term one and could only be carried out slowly. The ultimate objective was to place the three main groups, White, Coloured and Black, in their own residential areas in which they would eventually conduct their own affairs. Thus in their own areas the Natives and the Coloureds would find none of the colour bars of which they complained in the White areas. The dividing line would be 'vertical and not "horizontal" '.

The United Party accepted the principle of separation as the traditional policy of South Africa. It criticized the Apartheid plan as an impossible one which, even if it could be carried out, would be disastrous to industry. It declared that it was not in favour of assimilation of equality, and advocated (a) the maintenance of a policy of social and residential separation and the avoidance of racial intermixture, and (b) the development, while taking into account the differences between the races, of the Native people in their own and the country's interests. It refused to accept a purely negative policy of Apartheid based on depriving the Non-Europeans of their existing rights, which it said would lead to a Non-European nationalism hostile to the Europeans and the permanent interests of South Africa. It claimed that it stood for White leadership, which was essential not only in the true interests of the Europeans but also of the Non-Europeans in Southern Africa.

The United Party went to the polls in 1948 prepared to lose a few seats, yet convinced that they would again be returned to power. The result of the polling came as a great surprise to most people —even to the Nationalists. The National Party won eighty seats and the United Party sixty-four, while Labour won six. Thus the National Party had a majority of ten in the elected Chamber.

Smuts resigned without waiting for Parliament to meet, and Malan formed the first purely Afrikaner government in the history of the Union. For nearly forty years every Union Cabinet had contained at least one member of the English section of the population. Malan's Ministry was composed entirely of men of Afrikaner descent.

Dr. E. G. Jansen, who had been Speaker in the House of Assembly, was given the portfolio of Native Affairs, but in 1950 he resigned the position to become Governor-General. The portfolio was then accepted by Dr. H. F. Verwoerd (pronounced Fer-voot) upon whom fell the main responsibility for implementing the policy called Apartheid.

Verwoerd was born in Holland and brought to South Africa at the age of two. He was a brilliant scholar who studied at universities in Holland, Germany and the United States and was appointed head of the department of Sociology and Social Service at Stellenbosch University. He later undertook the editorship of a Nationalist paper in Johannesburg. Defeated when he stood for Parliament in 1948, he was given a seat in the Senate, where he was leader for the Malan Government.

When Verwoerd was made Minister of Native Affairs he explained 'the ultimate objective' of Apartheid to the representatives of the Natives. He insisted that there was no policy of repression in it, but the bringing into being of a position that had never before existed for the Native—that with full respect for his language, traditions, history and his various tribal groups he could proceed with his own development. He added that the foundations of a prosperous producing community must be laid in the Reserves, and Bantu agriculture must be organized on an economic basis. European industrialists would be encouraged to establish industries near to Native towns. Natives would then be able to reside in their own Native areas with their own schools, served by their own traders and governing themselves, and work in adjacent European areas. He added that in the European towns the residential areas of the Bantu, the Coloureds and the Indians would be separate. The object was to give them the largest measure of self-government possible in accordance with what the local authorities who built the townships were able to provide. Thus even in the European areas the Natives would not be isolated in order to oppress them but to enable them to form their own communities in which they could live full lives of work and service in all spheres.

The policy called Apartheid was welcomed by the Nationalists and by a large number of Afrikaner institutions.

In 1950 the Action Committee of the Dutch Reformed Churches presented a report to a conference at Bloemfontein which declared that equality in the same political and economic sphere could only lead to the submergence of the Whites by the Blacks. It found that there was only one way out of the difficulty—separate territories for Europeans and Non-Europeans. Each race would then be given every chance of development to the full.

Replying to those who advocated the continued gradual integration of White and Black on the same lines as in the past, the Action Committee declared that the Europeans could not continue to employ, educate and develop the Natives and at the same time restrict them to unskilled occupations. The Natives would fight for a say in the conduct of affairs and in their struggle would be supported from several quarters and from abroad. 'There remains,' asserted the Committee, 'no solution other than to separate the Natives completely in the long run.'

The South African Bureau of Race Relations (an Afrikaans society formed in 1949) issued a pamphlet in favour of Apartheid in which it argued that unless a policy of methodically reducing Native urbanization, combined with the development of the Reserves, was started at once it would be too late. The integration trend, it said, would become irreversible.

The Bureau devoted much time and study to the problem and reported that the policy of separate and distinctive development was the only one that guaranteed peace and safety for both the European and Native populations. It held that such a policy was practicable 'if the people of South Africa wish it'. The Bureau insisted, however, that the policy was a long-term one, and that it was absurd to maintain that a situation that had developed in the course of fifty years or more, and which was still in full swing, could be rectified in a few years.

Criticized for failing to estimate the cost of so vast a scheme, the Bureau retorted that 'if only the same amount were to be spent on the rehabilitation of the Native Reserves as was spent on the last war in South Africa—and within the same period—a large-scale development of the Reserves would be made possible'.

On the question of cost the Bureau reported: 'Once the process of development has been put into operation the Native areas themselves will be able to contribute progressively more to their own economic development. Naturally we shall have to assist them financially: but if South Africa is willing to spend millions yearly on the war in Korea, and on defence, we should certainly also be prepared to invest large sums of money in the development of the Native territories.'

In a paper read before an Afrikaans cultural society in Pretoria in June 1952, Professor N. J. J. Olivier, head of the Department of Bantu Studies at the Stellenbosch University, said that Africa as a whole 'would never be Europeanized even if millions of Europeans settled in the continent in the near future'. Africa's indigenous character would always be retained. The Europeans would always be very much in the minority. They might in some areas find themselves in a subordinate position with no share in the government of the territory. 'The only way out,' he went on, 'appears to be to have a new territorial division in the southern part of Africa into areas in which only European interests will be valid and others in which only the interests of the Natives will be considered.' He pointed out that leading people in South Africa advocated this arrangement and remarked: 'This seems to be the only expedient to satisfy both groups. If it is done the Native population will lose nothing, and the established European populations will be guaranteed security.'

The Malan Government's colour policy had a bad Press overseas, especially in the United Kingdom and the United States. The Prime Minister himself felt constrained to enter the lists in defence of Apartheid. The Rev. J. H. Piersma, of Grand Rapids, U.S.A., had written to him asking for 'a frank description of Apartheid' which he could use 'to convince the American public'.

Malan replied in a long letter in the course of which he said: 'It must be appreciated at the outset that Apartheid, separation, segregation or differentiation—whatever the name given to the traditional racial policy of South Africa—is part and parcel of the South African tradition as practised since the first Dutch settlement at the Cape in 1652, and is still supported by the large majority of White South Africans of the main political parties. The deep-rooted colour consciousness of the White South Africans—a phenomenon quite beyond the comprehension of the uninformed —arises from the fundamental difference between the two groups, White and Black. The difference in colour is merely the physical manifestation of the contrast between two irreconcilable ways of life, between barbarism and Christianity, and finally between overwhelming numerical odds on the one hand and insignificant numbers on the other. Such it was in the early beginnings, and such it largely remains. The racial differences are as pronounced today as they were three hundred years ago. Small wonder that the instinct of self-preservation is so inherent in the White South African. He has retained his identity all these years. He is not willing to surrender it now.'

Malan proceeded to explain the attitude of the Dutch Reformed Church on the Native question, and wrote: 'Passing then from the historical and spiritual basis of Apartheid to its everyday political application as practised by the present South African Government, let me remind you that government is the art of the possible. It makes no sense therefore to criticize the policy of Apartheid in the abstract and without due regard to facts and conditions as they exist and as they have been allowed to develop through the centuries. And, may I emphasize, that to consider only the rights of the Blacks would be precisely as immoral as to have regard only for the rights of the Whites. I must ask you to give White South Africans credit for not being a nation of scheming reactionaries imbued with base and inhuman motives, nor a nation of fools blind to the gravity of their vital problem. They are normal human beings. They are a small nation grappling with one of the most difficult problems in the world. To them millions of semi-barbarous Blacks look for guidance, justice and the Christian way of life. Here a tremendous experiment is being tried—not that fraught with the bloodshed of annihilation, nor that coloured by assimilation, but that inspired by a belief in logical differentiation with the acceptance of the basic human rights and responsibilities. Human rights and responsibilities can however only be exercised by human beings who are capable of appreciating their significance; and it is here that my Government, dealing as it does with a still primitive Non-White population, is faced with a major educational problem.'

He went on to recount the heavy and growing expenditure of the Union on education, housing and all manner of improvements made on behalf of the Non-Whites, and to explain the plans drawn up for the development of the Native Reserves. He closed his letter with these words: 'Theoretically, the object of the policy of Apartheid could be achieved by dividing the country into two parts with all the Whites in one and all the Blacks in the other. For the foreseeable future however this is simply not practical politics. Whether in time to come we shall reach a stage where some such division, say on a federal basis, will be possible, is a matter we must leave to the future. In any case the full implementation of the policy of separate racial development will take very many years. Call it an experiment if you like, and one could say it is an experiment which is as yet only in its initial stage. Many aspects of the problem are certainly far from clear and it would be unwise, even if it were possible, to draw up a blue-print for fifty years ahead. In more than one respect progress will have to be by trial and error. And if in the process we should err, I ask you and your countrymen not to judge our efforts only by our incidental failures nor to reproach us for what you may at this great distance judge as being lack of the spirit of Christ.'

On the publication of Malan's letter, the South African Institute of Race Relations wrote to him criticising much of his argument. 'What we regret in your statement,' the Institute remarked, 'is that it breathes an air of complacency, that its factual statements are unrelated to the total situation, that it above all gives no grounds for hope to the millions who are not in a Native Reserve. Your statement gives the impression that the Non-Whites of South Africa should be happy and contented: it fails to recognize the large number that have emerged from barbarism and heathenism and have earned a place in our society as civilized persons. Most unhappily it shows no understanding of the hopelessness and bitterness in the hearts of many of our people, or the mounting racial tension that threatens the peace of our country.'

The Apartheid policy was severely criticized in the United States where discrimination on the ground of colour was slowly being removed despite the fierce opposition of many communities in the Southern States.

Professor N. J. J. Olivier spent several months in America studying the colour question. He found that one of the main reasons for the sharp criticism of South Africa in that country arose from the fact that Americans identified the Union's Native problem with their Negro problem.

Professor Olivier insisted that the Union's Native problem could by no means be compared with the Negro question in the United States. The American Negro was, he said, in fact an American. He had no language and culture of his own, and where there was discrimination against him it arose purely from a colour basis. In South Africa the position was entirely different. Next to the race factor, which in his opinion was secondary, had to be borne in mind the fact that the Whites in South Africa would never be prepared to throw a cultural heritage of three hundred years to the wolves by adopting a policy of integration. Historically the South African pattern was the result of the Europeans' struggle for survival: the pattern in the United States was the result of the slave trade. Biologically the American Negro did not constitute a race; the Bantu did so. The numerical proportion of White to Black showed an inverse position in the two respective countries. The integration of the Negro in the United States represented an irrevocable and unchangeable tendency, and yet an immense measure of discrimination against the Negro was still to be found. In the United States the native Indians lived in Reserves, and the South African Bantu could in fact only be compared with them —not with the Negro.

Reviewing its defeat at the 1948 general election, the United Party leaders felt that Nationalist misrepresentation of the party's policy on the colour question had misled many voters. It was decided to prepare a statement showing clearly the attitude of the party. A nine-point policy was drafted covering the major issues before the country.

Point 4, which was headed 'White leadership with Justice', declared: 'The United Party stands for White leadership in South Africa as being essential in the true interests not only of the Europeans but also of the Non-Europeans. The United Party refuses to accept a purely negative policy of Apartheid. Leadership based merely on repression and depriving the Non-European of his existing rights will not only conflict with the pledges enshrined in the South Africa Act but will also cause resentment and estrangement, and ultimately lead to a Non-European nationalism hostile to the Europeans and the abiding interests of South Africa. The Party will bring about and maintain residential and social separation between the races of different colour, but accepts the fact that the Non-European is essential to the economic progress of South Africa and is entitled to his just reward. European civilization in Southern Africa can only be perpetuated by White leadership based upon principles of justice; by fully developing the sense of responsibility which arises from the intellectual and moral heritage of the European; and by pro- gressively strengthening the European population through selective immigration.'

The Roman Catholic bishops of South Africa decided unani- mously to maintain the church's stand against Apartheid.

The Anglican Church denounced Apartheid as un-Christian, and most of the Protestant churches held the same view. The Dutch Reformed Church, however, accepted the policy of separation of White and Non-White, and its mission work was organized on that basis.

The Native leaders rejected the idea of Apartheid and insisted that the mental attitude of the Whites towards the Non-Whites was entirely wrong. At a multi-racial conference the presidential address was delivered by the Rev. Z. R. Mahahane, the president of the Interdenominational African Ministers' Federation. He described the Government of the Union as a Whiteocracy formed by people who suffered from a twin psychological malady—fear complex and superiority complex. 'They do not seem,' he said, 'to believe in the personality of the Non-White man. To them he does not belong to the human race—he is not a descendant of Adam. Their concept of a Non-White person is that he is a "Kafir", a "Native", a "boy", a "girl", or a "maid", a sub-human, a member of a child race created by a benevolent Deity to serve the material interests of the superior race, the Herrenvolk, in the capacity of hewer of wood and drawer of water. The Coloured man is regarded as an appendage to the White man, and the Asian is regarded as an alien, a foreigner, an "uitlander", a temporary sojourner in a foreign land who cannot claim rights of citizenship in that country. I believe it is this faulty conception of the true nature of the Black man that is mainly responsible for this unfortunate mess in the government of the country coupled with this state of fear. Remove this combination of factors and all will be well.'

CHAPTER VII

Apartheid in Practice

Although to begin with the Malan Government had only a majority of ten in the elected Chamber it lost no time in implementing its colour policy by administrative action and legislative enactments.

There had never been a colour bar on the suburban railway lines in the Cape Peninsula. Within two months of becoming Minister of Transport, P. O. Sauer had portions of all trains reserved for Whites only.

In 1949 the Prohibition of Mixed Marriages Act was passed, which declared that a marriage between a European and a Non-European could not be solemnized. Dr. Donges, the Minister of the Interior, who was in charge of the measure, said that the object of the law was to check blood mixture and to promote racial purity.

In 1950 a law was passed imposing penalties for sexual intercourse between Europeans and Non-Europeans (who of course included the Coloureds). The Act of 1927 had applied to Europeans and Natives only. The new measure made it necessary for the captains of ships calling at South African ports to warn their crews against breaking the new law of the country. At first the Act was not very often enforced but later prosecutions increased. By 1957 there had been nearly 2,500 people convicted under it— and 1,176 of them were European men.

Verwoerd soon revealed himself as the most vigorous Minister of Native Affairs the country had ever had. He extended the scope and powers of his department and became the virtual ruler of an empire of ten million Black subjects. Within a few days of taking over the department he expounded his policy. He declared that the Nationalist Afrikaner was not an oppressor because he had known what it was to be oppressed.

'We know,' he said, 'what it means to fight for freedom and we realize that the Natives must also be given the opportunity to develop along their own lines under the guidance of the European instead of becoming imitators of the White man.' He went on to say that it was untrue that the Government did not want Non-Whites as allies. They did want them as their allies in order that there should be no bastard race, or blood bath, in the country later. He declared that the Natives who were race-conscious believed in Apartheid, and announced that a commission would be appointed to investigate the resources of the Reserves and ascertain how they could be developed within the next ten years.

This enquiry was the Commission for the Socio-Economic Development of the Bantu Areas within the Union of South Africa—a body which later became known more briefly as the Tomlinson Commission after the name of its chairman.

The activities of the Communists among the Non-Whites, especially the Natives, was watched with increasing anxiety by the Government. In 1950 it put through Parliament the Suppression of Communism Act. It began with a long and involved definition of Communism which may be quoted in full, for the text has often been discussed in courts of law and doubtless will be in the future. The Act defined Communism as meaning:

'The doctrine of Marxian socialism as expounded by Lenin or Trotsky, the Third Communist International or the Communist Information Bureau or any related form of that doctrine expounded or advocated in the Union for the promotion of the fundamental principles of that doctrine and includes in particular any doctrine or scheme

(a) which aims at the establishment of a despotic system of government based on the dictatorship of the proletariat under which one political organization only is recognized and all other political organizations are suppressed or eliminated: or

(b) which aims at bringing about any political industrial social or economic change within the Union by the promotion of disturbance or disorder by unlawful acts or omissions or by means which include the promotion of disturbance or disorder or such acts or omissions or threat: or

(c) which aims at bringing about any political industrial social or economic change within the Union in accordance with the directions or under the guidance of or in co-operation with any foreign or international institution whose purpose or one of whose purposes (professed or otherwise) is to promote the establishment within the Union of any political industrial social or economic system identical with or similar to any system in any country which has adopted a system of government such as is described in (a) or

(d) which aims at the encouragement of feelings of hostility between the European and non-European races of the Union the consequences of which are calculated to further the achievement of any object referred to in paragraph (a) or (b).

Under the Act a Communist is either a professed Communist or any person who, having been given a reasonable opportunity of making such representation as he may consider necessary, is deemed by the Governor-General to be a Communist on the ground that he is advocating defending or encouraging the achievement of any of the objects of Communism.

According to the Act it is a criminal offence punishable by imprisonment up to ten years to do any act likely to further the achievement of any of the objects of Communism, or to advocate, defend or encourage the achievement of such object or any act of omission likely to further its achievement.

The Act declared the Communist Party to be an unlawful organization, and also laid down that the Governor-General had the power to declare any other organization to be an unlawful organization. An organization becomes unlawful either because it falls within the definition of a Communist party or in consequence of a declaration by the Governor-General that he is satisfied that it is one or engages in activities calculated to further the objects of Communism. The Governor-General cannot be made to state the reason why he is satisfied that an organization is a communistic one.

When an organization is declared unlawful it is illegal for any person to remain a member of it. The assets of an unlawful organization are vested in a liquidator who is required to distribute any surplus, after winding it up, to charitable or scientific bodies nominated by the Minister.

The Minister has power to prohibit gatherings or individuals from attending gatherings of any kind if he has reason to believe that any one of the objects of Communism would be furthered at such a gathering. A convicted person can be removed from any area, or if not a South African by birth can be deported. Where a person has been convicted of knowingly allowing premises or property to be used in connection with offences under the Act, the court convicting him may declare his rights to such property to be forfeited to the State.

Under the Act the Minister appointed a liquidator to draw up a list of all persons who were officials, office-bearers, members or active supporters of the Communist Party at any time prior to or after the coming into operation of the Act. His task was rendered difficult because the Communist Party destroyed all its records. However, up to the end of 1955 some six hundred persons had been listed as Communists, and seventy-nine of them had been ordered by the Minister to resign from various trade unions. There were fifty-one prosecutions for breaking the law and the sentences imposed ranged from three to nine months' imprisonment. Two members of the Union House of Assembly—Sam Kahn and Brian Bunting—were ejected from Parliament under the Act.

The Malan Government also resolved to deal with the pass system, which had for many years been resented by Africans. The Natives complained that the police enforced the law harshly, and that people were arrested and fined or imprisoned for the most trivial infringement of the law made in ignorance. They said that they had to carry four or five different passes and that the loss of one of them involved them in penalties.

In 1942 a Parliamentary Committee known as the Smit Committee had reported that in the three northern Provinces between 1939 and 1941 there had been 348,907 arrests for contravention of the Pass Laws and in 318,858 cases convictions followed. 'These convictions,' stated the Committee, 'indicate the tremendous price which the country is paying in respect of these laws, for apart from the actual cost of administration there is the vast loss of labour due to detention during arrest and imprisonment. Fines constitute a drain on a Native's income which it has been shown it can ill afford. Apart from these considerations the harassing and constant interference with the freedom of movement of Natives gives rise to a burning sense of grievance and injustice which has an unsettling effect on the Native population as a whole. The application of these laws has also the undesirable feature of introducing large numbers of Natives to the machinery of criminal law and makes many familiar at an early age with prison. These laws create technical offences which involve little or no moral opprobrium. The Committee has reached the conclusion that rather than perpetuate the state of affairs described above it would be better to face the abolition of the Pass Laws.'

Owing to the exigencies of the Second World War the report of the Smit Committee was not acted upon and the old pass system remained in force.

In 1948, however, a memorandum was prepared dealing with the powers of the Provincial Councils and local authorities. It contained the following recommendation: 'An urgent and vital necessity exists for the institution of what might, for the sake of convenience, be called a "national register" of all the inhabitants of the Union irrespective of race, colour or group, the responsibility for which should rest solely on the Union Government.' It was pointed out that such registers existed in other countries and there seemed to be no sound reason why there should not be one in South Africa. Its usefulness was stressed, and the memorandum declared: 'It is not expected that the public will object to a national register if its purpose is clearly understood. The Provinces therefore recommend its introduction.'

At this time the Malan Government was considering the implementation of its Apartheid policy, under which it was obvious that some official classification of the population on the basis of colour was essential. There were many border-line cases in which it was difficult to decide whether an individual was a European or a Non-European, or whether a man was a Coloured person or a Native.

In 1950 therefore the Government put through Parliament the Population Registration Act which provided for the compilation of a register of the entire population of the Union classified as White, Coloured or Native, and for the issue of identity cards to persons whose names were on the roll. The measure was opposed by the United Party, but the third reading in the House of Assembly was passed by 63 votes to 56.

The classifying of the entire population on the basis of colour revealed many tragic cases. Some members of a family were held to be White and others coloured. A boy of fourteen hanged himself because he was ordered to attend a Coloured school while his brother was classed as White and went to a White school. A European couple adopted a baby who as it grew older proved to be Coloured. They were told to send the child to a Coloured institution, and rather than do so they left the country and took the child with them. A man who has married a Coloured girl found that it was an offence for them to live together, and they too went overseas. A Special Board was set up to which appeals could be made, for by May 1957 one hundred thousand border-line cases had been encountered.

This Act was followed in 1952 by a law repealing all the Pass Laws and providing instead for the issuing to Natives of a 'reference book' containing information regarding their identity. Thus it was claimed that Native would in future only have to carry one document, which would be virtually the same as the one to be issued to the Whites and the Coloureds. Any Native not in possession of a 'reference book' might be fined or imprisoned.

In some urban centres there were Whites and Non-Whites living side by side. The Government decided to deal with this intermingling on a national scale. In 1950 it placed before Parliament the Group Areas Bill, which Malan said was the most important of all the Apartheid measures. It set up machinery by which separate areas could be marked off for residence, occupation and trade for the different racial groups. Any radial group could then be moved from the area it occupied and placed in another area reserved exclusively for it.

The Bill was introduced by the Minister of the Interior (Dr. Donges) who explained that the law did not itself demarcate areas for each racial group. It created the machinery for doing so over a period of years and 'in a fair, equitable and judicial manner'. Every part of the country became a 'controlled area': and specific areas would be assigned to Whites, Coloureds and Natives, though in the case of the two last-named the areas could be subdivided. Once an area was demarcated for a particular group there could be no transfer of ownership or occupation without a permit. A Land Tenure Advisory Board would demarcate the areas; but no area could be proclaimed except with the approval of both Houses of Parliament. Within the proclaimed areas there would be a certain amount of self-government for the residents under the control of the Government. There would be no compensation for those removed, though the sale of their land would give a fair return to owners who had to transfer to another area.

Dr. Donges claimed that the measure would be advantageous in that new avenues of employment would be opened for each group.

He declined to refer the Bill to a Select Committee on the ground that a clear cut principle was laid down which could not be modified, and because there was already sufficient evidence on the matter without hearing more witnesses. He asserted that the Bill realized one of the main objects of Apartheid, namely the elimination of friction between races in the Union, by providing separate areas for the different races. It would be a gradual process, and some measure of inconvenience and sacrifice was unavoidable, but in the end the plan would be for the benefit of all. The principle of separation had already been accepted and applied in some places. Voluntary action could not, however, achieve the results desired, and compulsion was necessary.

The United Party accepted the principle of separation as the traditional policy of the country, though it argued that the Bill would do more harm than good. Its leader (J. G. N. Strauss) moved an amendment declaring that the House declined to pass the Bill before a commission of enquiry presided over by a judge had reported upon it. He argued that the measure would lower the prestige of South Africa in the eyes of the world, would upset the property market and create uncertainty for a long period. It would also interfere with testamentary dispositions and undermine the rights of mortgagees.

The Labour Party tabled another amendment demanding the provision of alternative accommodation for the people moved, and compensation for the owners of property.

The Native representatives strongly condemned the measure as harsh and unjust, saying that it would result in great hardship for many people and would create more friction between the races instead of eliminating it.

Speaking in the third reading debate Dr. Donges said: 'We believe that if we remove the points of contact that cause friction, then we will remove the possibility of that friction and we will be able to prevent the conflagration which might one day break out. This is what the Bill stands for . . . Its object is to ensure racial peace . . . It has been introduced because we do not believe that the future of South Africa will be that of a mixed population, and this is one measure, and one of the major measures, designed to preserve White South Africa while at the same time giving justice and fair play to the Non-Europeans in this country.'

The third reading was carried by 73 votes to 58, whereas the second reading had been carried by only 69 votes to 61.

Protests against the Group Areas Act were not confined to Non-White organizations. The Methodist and Anglican churches condemned the measure, and the Labour Party asked the Government to suspend the enforcement of the Act. The Institute of Race Relations sent a deputation to the Government pleading for more lenient treatment of the communities likely to be affected. The Johannesburg City Council made numerous efforts to secure some modification in the application of the Act.

At a meeting in Johannesburg in February 1957, the Bishop of Johannesburg, the Rt. Rev. Ambrose Reeves, described the implementation of the Group Areas Act as 'a refined method of mental torture which only those who have to endure it can ever fully understand.' He said that the enforcement of the law would mean that some nine thousand Indians, seven hundred Chinese, some seven thousand five hundred Coloureds and two thousand Malays would have to leave areas where for years they had lived, worked and traded. The Bishop described the legislation as 'part and parcel of the tendency so obvious in these days to put the whole of life in this country into a strait-jacket in obedience to the dictates of the prevailing racial sectarianism.'

The Nationalists were not moved by these arguments. They insisted that the Europeans who wanted to preserve the European race and the European way of life were entitled to erect barriers to safeguard themselves.

Speaking at a joint sitting of both Houses of Parliament in 1954, Malan said that the leader of the Labour Party held that numbers alone must count and that everyone must be thrown into the same pot and boiled down together into one and the same substance or mixture. He went on: 'What I want to say in this regard is that basically it is tantamount to a charge on his part against the Creator. The question that he put, although he did not express it in so many words, is this: 'Why did the Creator make the mistake of creating countries, nations and languages? He should not have done so. He set mankind a task which it is impossible—the task of destroying His work again. Why did He not, instead of allowing such an assortment to come into existence, rather make the world a flat level plain, as level as a table? Then all those difficulties and those barriers would not have existed today. But He proceeded to create the world in such a way, with the various places of abode of mankind, that it is impossible to have anything but different countries and different languages, and in addition to that the Creator also proceeded to create different colours. No, I say that basically it is really a charge against Creation and against the Creator.'

The application of the principle of Apartheid raised numerous minor issues. In the Transvaal and the Cape two Bantu had been called to the Bar. The one in the Transvaal wished to take advocate's chambers in the building in which the European advocates had their chambers and to use the common room provided. The European advocates did not object; but the Government used the Group Areas Act to prevent the Native lawyer having chambers in the same building as the Whites. In the Supreme Court in Cape Town a special robing-room was provided for Non-European advocates who had previously used the general-robing room with the approval of the majority of the European advocates. Non-European advocates had to have their chambers in the location. In a magistrate's court in the Transvaal a Native lawyer was not allowed to sit at the same table as the White lawyers.

An important change in Native administration was made by the Bantu Authorities Act of 1951 which replaced governmental institutions on the European model, elected under the Native Affairs Act of 1920, by a system of tribal government. Under the former system there were Native councils in the Transkei and Native Reserve Boards in other areas with limited powers of spending money.

The new Act provided for the setting up of tribal authorities for tribes or communities, and above them regional authorities, and at the apex of the system a Bantu territorial authority. A Bantu tribal authority consisted of the chief or headman and the tribal councillors. All these tribal authorities could pay revenue into a treasury and provide schools, dams and bridges and generally improve their area. The Act abolished the Natives Representative Council.

The most important Native authority under the old system had been the Transkeian Territories General Council, usually called the Bunga. It had 103 members, two-thirds of whom were elected, who ruled over a million and a half Natives in the five Transkeian territories. In 1952 the Bunga refused to accept the new Act. Verwoerd then visited the territories and explained the working of the new system which he said increased the powers of the chiefs and the headmen and gave tribal authorities more scope for putting through betterment schemes of all kinds. As a result of the Minister's visit the Bunga in 1955 decided to abolish itself by agreeing unanimously to replace its 26 districts by tribal authorities under the new Act. The Bunga had been in existence for fifty years. In its final resolution it declared that it accepted the principle of the Bantu Authorities Act 'in order to preserve the solidarity of the Transkei'.

The Malan Government also decided to review the whole system of Native education. For a great many years schools for the Bantu had been provided by the missionary societies which the local governments subsidized and so maintained a certain measure of control. In 1939 the Hertzog Government drafted a Native Education Bill which placed Bantu education under the control of the Central Government. The outbreak of the Second World War and the defeat of the Government ensued and the Bill was dropped.

In 1949 after the Malan Government came into power the Native Education Commission was appointed. It sat for two years and consulted Native organisations all over the country. In its report it held that the aim of Native education should be two-fold: (1) From the viewpoint of the whole society the aim should be the development of a modern progressive culture with social institutions which will be in harmony with one another and with the evolving conditions of life to be met in South Africa; (2) From the viewpoint of the individual the aim should be the development of character and intellect and the equipping of the child for his future work and surroundings.

Backed by this report the Government placed before Parliament the Bantu Education Bill of 1953 under which the State assumed control of Bantu education and proposed to take over all the existing mission school buildings.

With the exception of the Dutch Reformed Churches most of the churches protested strongly against the measure. Some of them agreed to transfer their school buildings to the Government, feeling that there was nothing else to be done as their schools could not be carried on without a government grant. Others declined to fall in with the scheme and raised money to attempt to carry on as before, under permission from the Government. The Act laid down that no school for Natives could be opened without the consent of the Minister of Native Affairs.

In defending the Bantu Education Act, Verwoerd said: 'What is the use of subjecting a Native child to a curriculum which in the first instance is traditionally European ? What is the use of teaching the Bantu child mathematics when it cannot use it in practice? That is quite absurd. Education must train and teach people in accordance with their opportunities in life according to the sphere in which they live.' He told Parliament that the Government would give the Natives a fundamental education—the three R's, a mother tongue, and English and Afrikaans up to Standard II. The Native parents would be given a say in the control of education. There were about 2,500,000 Native children of school-going age of whom 900,000 attended some 5,500 schools staffed by 20,000 teachers. The expense was about £8 million a year. With two sessions daily of about three hours several hundred thousand more Native children could be taught. There were about thirty industrial schools which taught manual training to Natives. He assured the Natives that the education given would not be inferior. It would enable Natives to become doctors, parsons and teachers and so on and to serve their own people. The churches would have free access to the schools to give religious instruction.

The Native representatives in Parliament opposed the measure arguing that it deprived the African people of the services of those who would willingly assist them in their struggle for education. They said that the Bill 'put the whole field of Bantu education into a strait-jacket.' The Bill was passed by 63 votes to 37.

The British Council of Churches in Britain condemned the Act which it declared 'was intended to ensure the mental as well as the physical segregation of the Bantu and to deny them any place in the European community above the level of certain forms of labour.'

The Government denied that this was so, and a statement issued by the Under-Secretary for Bantu Education contained the following: 'Academic education will still be available and there is no intention of decreasing the number of secondary schools in the country, of which there are approximately two hundred at the moment. The tendency will be for these schools to increase in number as the demand for the services of the educated Bantu in the service of his people grows. On the other hand there are numbers of students, just as in any other country in the world, who are unable because of their lack of capacity to benefit by an academic course. Technical education will be made available for them.' The statement declared that all the talk about lowering standards and limiting facilities arose from 'ignorance, prejudice and hysteria on the part of those people who should know better.'

The Nationalists also advocated the application of the principle of separation to the universities. There were nine in the Union and four of them did not admit Non-Europeans. Two others were not closed to Non-Whites though there was a certain amount of separation in teaching and in social activities. The universities of Cape Town and the Witwatersrand on the other hand were open. They admitted Non-Europeans to the same lectures and the same student societies as the Europeans. In 1954 Cape Town had 271 Non-White students and the Witwatersrand had 214.

At several National Party congresses resolutions had been passed calling for the separation of Whites and Non-Whites at all the universities, and Malan had made the change one of the planks in his 1948 election platform. In 1952 he said at Stellenbosch that the universities 'ought to bear the same characteristics as the State itself which called them into being and upon which they were financially dependent . . . and because separate schools for Europeans and Non-Europeans are the tradition and general policy of the land, and the situation of mixing in certain universities is a blatant anomaly.'

A commission was appointed 'to investigate and report on the practicability and financial implications of providing separate training facilities for Non-Europeans at universities'. The Government was not satisfied with the commission's report and set up a departmental committee to investigate the subject. Then came the 1953 general election and the matter was dropped and no direct action was taken during Malan's Prime Ministership.

Meanwhile the African National Congress had decided to adopt a policy of uncompromising non-co-operation with the Government. It boycotted the Natives Representative Council, all the Native Advisory Boards and the election of Europeans to represent the Natives in Parliament.

It also established closer relations with the South African Indian National Congress, and the two bodies declared a one-day strike on May 1, 1951, as a protest against discriminatory laws. The authorities tried to protect non-strikers against intimidation, and there were clashes with the police in which eighteen Non-Europeans were killed. The loss of life was commemorated on June 26 when there was a united conference of Non-Whites to decide upon future policy. Since then, June 26 has been regarded as an important day in the Non-White calendar and it has been made the starting point for several movements.

When the African National Congress met in 1951 the grievances of the Africans were proclaimed in strong terms. The President, Dr. Moroka, said that they fought not against people but against the iniquity of the laws by which they were ruled. They were prepared to fight for the welfare of South Africa, but only upon terms of equal partnership. Any terms which were designed to relegate them to the position of an inferior they scorned and would stoutly reject.

W. W. Bopape, the secretary of the Transvaal Executive Committee of the A.N.C., was reported to have expressed the hope that the Congress would decide what action was necessary to take over the government of the country immediately. The Congress, he said, had arrived at the stage where it no longer asked for improvements but asked that it should control the country because the Natives were in the majority. The Non-Europeans had been under European domination in South Africa for a hundred years. 'Are we prepared to endure another ten years of it?' he demanded; and according to the newspaper reports there were 'loud shouts of "No" and wild cheering'.

The conference unanimously resolved to call upon the Government to repeal the Pass Laws, the Stock Limitation Act, the Suppression of Communism Act of 1950, the Group Areas Act of 1950, the Bantu Authorities Act of 1951 and the Voters Act of 1951 by not later than February 1952, 'failing which the African National Congress will hold protest demonstrations and meetings on April 6 as a prelude to the implementation of a plan for the defiance of unjust laws'.

The Indian National Congress had decided to take similar action and a Joint Planning Council was set up by the two bodies to arrange details of the passive resistance campaign.

The reasons for launching the defiance movement were set out in two letters addressed to the Prime Minister direct.

One was from the African National Congress and was signed by Dr. Moroka and W. M. Sisula (Secretary-General). It stated that the Congress had since its establishment endeavoured by every constitutional means to bring to the notice of the Government the legitimate demands of the African people and had repeatedly pressed in particular their inherent right to be represented in

Parliament, Provincial and municipal councils and all councils of State. This attitude was a demonstration not only of the willingness and readiness of the African people to co-operate with the Government but also evidence of their sincere desire for peace, harmony and friendship among all sections of the population.

The letter proceeded: 'As is well known, the Government through its repressive policy of trusteeship, segregation and Apartheid and through legislation that continues to insult and degrade the African people by depriving them of fundamental human rights enjoyed in all democratic communities, have categorically rejected our offer of co-operation. The consequence has been the gradual worsening of the social, economic and political position of the African people and a rising tide of bitterness and tension.'

After enumerating the Acts to which objection was taken the letter went on: 'The cumulative effect of this legislation is to crush the national organizations of the oppressed people; to destroy the economic position of the people and create a reservoir of cheap labour for the farms and the gold mines; to prevent the unity and development of the African people towards full nationhood and to humiliate them in a host of other matters. The African National Congress as the national organization of the African people cannot remain quiet on an issue that is a matter of life and death to the people; to do so would be a betrayal of the trust and confidence placed upon it by the African people.'

Having called upon the Government to repeal all discriminatory legislation by February 29, 1952, the letter concluded: 'We firmly believe that the freedom of the African people, the elimination of the exploitation of man by man and the restitution of democracy, liberty and harmony in South Africa are such vital and fundamental matters that the Government and the Public must know that we are fully resolved to achieve them in our life-time. The struggle which our people are about to begin is not directed against any race or national group but against the unjust laws which keep in perpetual subjection and misery vast sections of the population. In this connection it is a source of supreme satisfaction to us to know that we have the full support and sympathy of enlightened and honest men and women, Black and White, in our country and across the seas and that the present tension and crisis have been brought about not by the African leaders but by the Government themselves. We are instructed to point out that we have taken this decision in full appreciation of the consequences it entails, and we emphasize that whatever reaction is provoked from certain circles in this country posterity will judge that the action we are about to begin was in the interests of all in our country and will inspire our people for long ages to come. We desire to place on record that for our part we have endeavoured over the last forty years to bring about conditions for genuine progress and true democracy.'

The second letter to the Prime Minister was sent by the South African Indian Congress. It denounced various measures passed by the Government and went on: 'The policy of Apartheid is anti-democratic, reactionary and contrary to the laws of natural development of history and can only be imposed by means of Fascist tyranny and unrestrained dictatorship. Indeed not only have the Non-European people become the victims of this policy but it has also encroached upon the rights and liberties of the European people as evidenced by State interference with the freedom of individuals to travel abroad, with the freedom of the right of parents regarding their children's education, with the freedom of the Press, and with the freedom of trade unions to conduct their own affairs. It is a fact of history that since your Government came into power it has attempted to impose its Apartheid policy with callous disregard for the feelings of the people and disastrous consequences to the country as a whole. Race relations have reached the most critical stage in our country's history. There has been unbridled incitement of race animosity and prejudice between the different population groups and unremitting race propaganda. There has been a steady increase in the use of violence and intimidation by the police and the occurrence of race riots hitherto unknown. There has been a constant tendency to place unlimited and arbitrary powers in the hands of Ministers, powers which under the provisions of the various laws enacted by your Government are being used to crush the rights and liberties particularly of the Non-European people.'

Malan replied only to the African National Congress, and he did so in a letter signed by his Private Secretary. He said that it should be clearly understood that the Government would under no circumstances entertain the idea of giving administrative, or executive or legislative powers over Europeans, or within a European community, to Bantu men and women. The Government therefore had no intention of repealing the long existing laws differentiating between European and Bantu.

Malan went on to say that the offer of co-operation by the Congress was not a genuine one, but an attempt to embark on the first steps towards supplanting European rule in the course of time. 'Racial harmony,' he said, 'cannot be attained in this manner. Compliance with such demands must inevitably lead to disaster for all population groups. Not only temporary racial tension, due to misunderstanding, but worse would follow and the Bantu would suffer first and most. For instance if the latter were to be exposed to full competition without their present protection they would soon lose the land now safeguarded and being increased for them. The masses would suffer misery indeed if they lost the many privileges which the Union of South Africa—in contrast to other countries—provides for them. They would pay the price in order to satisfy the political ambitions of the few who are prepared to tear loose from the background of their own nation. The road to peace and goodwill lies in the acceptance of the fact that separate population groups exist, and in giving each group the opportunity of developing its ambitions and capacities in its own area or within its own community on its own lines in the service of its own people. . . . It should be clearly understood that while the Government is not prepared to grant the Bantu political equality within the European community it is only too willing to encourage Bantu initiative, Bantu services and Bantu administration within the Bantu community, and there to allow the Bantu people full scope for their potentialities.'

The letter concluded by warning the Bantu that if they defied law and order the Government would 'make full use of the machinery at its disposal to quell any disturbances and thereafter deal adequately with those responsible for initiating subversive activities of any nature whatever'.

The African National Congress replied to the Prime Minister's letter at considerable length. It said that the Reserve land policy had always been designed to protect European rather than African land rights, and that even within the so-called Reserves Africans held only occupancy privileges at the discretion of the Government and these Reserves were notoriously congested and over-crowded. The so-called rehabilitation scheme had aggravated the misery of the people and rendered thousands destitute and homeless and had exposed them to vexatious regimentation by Native Commissioners and petty Trust officials.

The Congress added: 'With reference to the campaign of mass

action which the A.N.C. intends to launch, we would point out that as a defenceless and voteless people we have explored other channels without success. The African people are left with no alternative but to embark upon the campaign referred to. We desire to state emphatically that it is our intention to conduct this campaign in a peaceful manner, and that any disturbances, if they must occur, will not be of our making.'

To prepare their followers for the campaign, the Non-European leaders addressed meetings all over the country. Their speeches stressed the miserable and humiliating conditions under which the Non-Whites lived compared with the freedom and prosperity enjoyed by the Whites. One of the speakers exclaimed: 'You who today work in the mines, you who today work on the farms, you who today build a beautiful road for the motor cars, you are the people who are hungry, you are the people who have no clothes, you are the people who must live under pass laws, you are the people who are oppressed in this country. If they put you in jail I ask you: Is your condition any better outside?'

Sometimes the oratory assumed a more minatory form as when one speaker said: 'I want to tell the White man that there are a hundred and fifty million of us in the continent of Africa. And in the continent of Africa there are only three million White people. When the army of freedom marches forward it will brush aside three million White people.'

As it was intended to conduct a non-violence campaign, volunteers were especially trained for the part they had to play. They were taught the methods of passive resistance adopted in India, warned that they might be roughly handled, and made to take an oath that under no circumstances would they retaliate with violence.

The defiance campaign began on June 26 and lasted into October.

Disobedience took the form of going out at night without a pass; entering a location without a permit; using railway coaches, waiting rooms and platform seats marked for Europeans only; entering the European section of the post office, and so on. In some cases the resisters told the police in advance exactly what they were going to do and when they were going to do it. When arrested and charged in court they pleaded guilty and used the dock as a platform from which to proclaim their complaints against the Government and the whole discriminatory system. They refused to pay fines and went to prison.

As the campaign lengthened the courts imposed heavier penalties. Resisters entering the 'For Whites Only' doors at the railway station in Johannesburg were sent to prison for two months with hard labour. Some of the volunteers under the age of twenty-one were ordered to be whipped.

The Government also struck at the organizations behind the campaign. Twenty leading men in the African National Congress and the Indian National Congress were arrested and charged under the Suppression of Communism Act with having 'advocated' advised or encouraged a scheme which aimed at the bringing about of political, industrial, social or economic changes within the Union by means which included unlawful acts or omission or the threat of such acts or omission'. They were found guilty and received suspended sentences under which they were restricted in their movements and attendance at meetings.

A few Europeans took an active part in the defiance campaign. Patrick Duncan, a son of the former Governor-General of the Union, Sir Patrick Duncan, marched with a procession into the Germiston location and was fined £100 or 100 days' imprisonment with hard labour. He went to prison and remained there for fourteen days. Then his fine was paid and he was released. Several European women who took part in the campaign served sentences of twenty-five days' imprisonment.

The idea was to fill the jails to overflowing and make it impossible to punish all the offenders. In five months some eight thousand Natives and Indians were sent to prison.

Although the campaign had been launched on the basis of non-violence it led to large gatherings of sympathising Natives and rioting broke out in several locations. At Port Elizabeth four Whites were killed and buildings were burnt and motor cars and other property damaged. At East London two Whites were murdered, one of them being a Catholic missionary nun who had for years worked among the people of the Native location. She was burnt to death when her car was set on fire and her body was mutilated.

The leaders of the African National Congress charged the Government and the police with the responsibility for the riots. They alleged that the police opened fire with fatal effects before a single European had been injured. They asked for a public inquiry into the outbreaks. The Government did not think it necessary to hold one.

The Government however took additional powers to enable it

to deal more effectively with passive resistance campaigns. As soon as Parliament met in 1953 it put through the Criminal Law Amendment Act, one clause of which laid down that 'any person who in any way whatsoever advises, encourages, incites, commands, aids or procures any other person or persons in general or uses any language calculated to cause any other person or persons in general to commit an offence by way of protest against a law . . . shall be guilty of an offence'.

The Act provided that a person convicted of an offence committed by way of protest or in support of a campaign against a law or in support of a campaign for the repeal or modification, variation or limitation of the application or administration of a law might be punished in a magistrate's court by a fine of £300 or three years' imprisonment. In the case of a second or subsequent conviction the court could not impose a fine without at the same time imposing a whipping or imprisonment. The property of a convicted person could be sold for the purpose of paying the fine imposed, so that it would not be possible for a convicted person to elect to go to prison to avoid the payment of a fine. The law also provided that any person convicted of advising or encouraging any person to commit an offence by way of protest against a law might be sentenced to five years' imprisonment and a whipping of ten strokes.

Owing to the rioting and the heavier penalties provided under the new law, the Joint Planning Council of the two Congresses finally decided to call off the defiance campaign.

The resistance movement had the sympathy of the Liberals among the Europeans. They however were few in number, and probably the majority of the Whites were prepared to back the Government in any measures it thought necessary to defeat the malcontents.

The struggle took place, too, within a few months of the general election of 1953, and naturally it was used by the Government in its appeal to the public to give it ample backing in its fight against disruptive forces.

The United Party made a determined effort to reverse the result of the 1948 appeal to the country. Smuts had died in 1950, and the new leader of the party was J. G. N. Strauss, who directed the preparation of a thirty-page pamphlet outlining the party's policy on a variety of subjects.

The party denounced Apartheid as envisaged by the Government as likely to worsen the relations between Black and White and to hamper industrial expansion. It accepted economic integration as a necessary dynamic process that would continue, because the integration of Bantu labour in the Union's economy simply meant that Bantu labour was essential to that economy. The party, however, regarded it as a necessary task to 'regulate, guide and control economic integration according to the reasonable demands of our economic life and the best interests of South Africa'. Uncontrolled economic integration would be dangerous and might lead to inefficiency and 'a great aggravation of social problems'. Too rapid integration would lead to friction and conflict which would hamper the achievement of co-operation.

The United Party held that the indiscriminate throwing together of people on the basis of so-called equality of rights in all spheres of life, irrespective of the differences in outlook and civilization, was bound to lead to conflicts to the detriment of all. 'From the point of view of practical statesmanship,' it declared, 'a measure of differentiation might reflect a more realistic and enlightened approach under present conditions. Discrimination or differentiation is not necessarily an evil. The all-important question is the basis on which it is done and the motive behind it. Accordingly the party accepts the basic principle of urban and influx control as laid down in the Native Areas Act as being in the interests of both Whites and Bantu.'

The United Party accepted the colour bar in industry but believed that the economic interests of the White worker could best be safeguarded by agreement between labour and management on wage rates and the classification of particular jobs. It recognized that claims for the extension of political rights were an inevitable historical corollary to an increase in economic power. It recognized that the Bantu must be trained in democratic responsibilities, and that as they moved towards the acquisition of Western standards of civilization their acceptance of a greater share in the administration of the country would be essential for the maintenance of inter-racial harmony. The United Party therefore proposed greater responsibility for the Bantu in their own areas to give them experience of domestic administration. It would establish bodies at different levels through which the Bantu 'can maintain liaison with existing instruments of government'.

The United Party entered into an agreement with the Labour Party to obviate the splitting of the anti-Nationalist vote. It claimed it was fighting in defence of the constitution and the liberty of the individual against a party with totalitarian tendencies.

The Nationalists stood firmly on their Apartheid policy and the need for safeguarding the supremacy of the White race. They pointed to the defiance campaign as showing how essential it was to have a strong Government in office.

The United Party was fairly confident of success. The public expected a very close finish.

But the National Party won an outstanding victory. The final figures were: National Party 94; United Party 57; Labour Party 5. Counting the Native representatives on the side of the Opposition the Malan Government had a majority of twenty-nine over all possible combinations against it. The Government regarded the result of the election as a new and stronger vote of confidence in its plans for implementing the policy of Apartheid. Further measures sanctioning discrimination on the ground of the colour of the skin were laid before Parliament.

For many years the railways and municipal and other bodies had provided separate accommodation for White and Black. In several cases in which Non-Europeans had been prosecuted for defying the regulations the courts had held that the waiting-rooms and other amenities reserved for Non-Europeans must not be materially inferior to those set apart for Europeans. In 1953 the Government put through the Reservation of Separate Amenities Act which laid down that when a separate amenity was provided for a particular race it was unnecessary to provide a substantially similar amenity for any other race. It gave power for the reservation of seats, counters, premises and vehicles for the exclusive use of different races, and made it an offence for a person wilfully to use an amenity not allocated to his particular race. This law gave for the first time statutory power to the owners of hotels, theatres, etc., to exclude persons on the ground of race or colour.

Malan viewed with concern the change in the composition of the old British Empire. New Dominions were becoming members of it, whose attitude might, he felt, ultimately affect the relations of the Union with the Commonwealth.

In an interview he pointed out that the then British Colonial Secretary (Mr. Griffiths) had welcomed in advance the new Gold Coast Negro State (Ghana) as a member of the Commonwealth and had also announced the policy of converting the British colonies one after the other into free and independent members of the Commonwealth, presumably on an equal footing in every respect with the existing Commonwealth countries. This was followed by a prediction by Mr. Gordon Walker, the British Secretary for Commonwealth Relations, that the admission of the Gold Coast would be followed by the islands of the West Indies.

Malan said that this policy would certainly not end there. 'We must expect,' he remarked, 'that the series of new Commonwealth members will soon be completed by the addition of other territories like India-controlled East Africa, and Uganda and Nyasaland, to speak only of Africa.'

'There we have,' Malan went on, 'a glaring anomaly in existing Commonwealth Relations. The Commonwealth is a closed group, all free and all equal, and consequently one would expect that in admitting a new member all would have an equal say because it might affect the whole character of the group. But what do we find? Acting on her own, and without consultation with, or the approval of, the other members, Britain recently admitted India, Pakistan and Ceylon to the Commonwealth and now intends to continue the process without restriction and in the same way. It is true that as colonies the territories belong to Britain alone; but as prospective members of the Commonwealth there are others who have just as much interest in their position and who should have an equal say whether they should be admitted or not. This anomaly should be removed without delay.'

'The position,' continued Malan, 'is this. The Commonwealth can, and could in the past, exist only as a result of a feeling of solidarity among all its members. And this feeling of solidarity can, and could, exist only on the basis of two things—namely, specific common interests and a sufficient homogeneity of cultural and political outlook. The bond of common kinship on which so much reliance was placed would not appear to be strong enough —as in the case of Ireland, India and Burma—and in any case it is too distant and vague a thing to exercise any real force in the long run. As far as the Commonwealth as a whole is concerned it has become a symbol separated from the fulfilment of any constitutional function. When the Commonwealth consisted only of five members—Britain, Canada, Australia, South Africa and New Zealand—the position was simple because the conditions for solidarity were still present, namely, common interests and the necessary homogeneity. But now as a result of the new, and especially the latest, events and declarations of policy, the question must necessarily arise: What greater solidarity or common interests or homogeneity does there exist for example between South Africa and India than exists between South Africa and Holland, or Belgium, or France or Germany; or for example between Australia and the Negro State of West Africa than between Australia and the United States ? To this question there can only be one answer.'

Asked how he would summarize the position. Malan replied: 'Like this: The recently announced policy of the British Government means nothing less than an undermining of the foundations of the Commonwealth and its gradual liquidation. Between the United Nations, which with its policy of intervention makes it possible through that organization for one Commonwealth country to interfere in the domestic affairs of another, and the new British Commonwealth policy, the Commonwealth itself cannot last. We who attach value to its continued existence may deeply regret it, but unfortunately the fault is not ours. In conclusion I would say: For South Africa the situation offers nothing good, and for this reason even circles who differ greatly from one another are doubtfully shaking their heads. May it bring the two White races closer together. On their consolidation on a sound basis of national unity lies our common salvation.'

Malan, speaking in Parliament, alluded to the decision of the British Government to give self-government to the Gold Coast and said that the step taken was a disastrous one for Africa and the Union, and its repercussions would not be confined to the Gold Coast. He added that the Union must establish a good understanding with the Rhodesias, for they must all stand together 'for the maintenance of Western Christian civilization'.

The Malan Government continued to have a bad Press overseas. Its discriminatory legislation on the ground of colour was widely criticized, and members of the Union Cabinet protested that the attacks were unfair because the Union's case was not understood and little or no newspaper space was given to presenting it.

Among the Union's measures that were strongly condemned abroad was its decision to hire out prison labour. The Government put into operation a plan under which groups of farmers were allowed to build prisons in the rural areas which were then used for the hiring out of prisoners as labourers for the farmers.

Only Natives sentenced to six months or under were sent to the farm prisons, and the farmers paid two shillings a day to those who agreed to work for them.

The Minister of Justice (Mr. C. R. Swart) explained that the object of the scheme was to keep short-term petty offenders out of the ordinary gaols in order to protect them from contact with hardened prisoners. No prisoner was to be released as a farm worker without his full and free consent, and the superintendent of the prison had to satisfy himself that the farmer to whom prisoners were released was a fit and proper person to be entrusted with prison labour. The farmer had to provide the prisoner with food and accommodation on a par with his ordinary servants, and in addition medical attention when necessary.

The farm prison plan was singled out in numerous overseas papers as an example of the methods of a Nazified State. Yet as a matter of fact the hiring of convicts as labourers had been common in South Africa for sixty years. When the Cape was a British colony in 1889 the De Beers Company had a private prison at Kimberley holding two thousand convicts. Some of the Rand gold mines employed convicts, and private prisons were built in the rural areas when General Smuts was Prime Minister.

In the Transvaal however there were complaints that the system was abused. It was said that lower grade officials acted as agents for the land-owners and sent men to the farms before they had been brought before a court and sentenced. Natives suddenly vanished from their families and were found weeks or months afterwards working on farms from which they were unable to escape. Cases before the courts showed that Natives had been severely beaten on farms and that several of them had died. The labourers alleged that they were worked long hours with insufficient food and were sjambokked if they did not work fast enough. They were locked up at night and if they ran away were pursued and thrashed. In some cases farmers and their boss-boys were charged with manslaughter and even murder. The Government ordered an investigation into the system and finally stopped the recruiting of Union Natives for farms, though apparently foreign Natives were still offered work in the rural areas through official channels.

The clearing of the slum areas in Johannesburg, and the compulsory removal of their inhabitants, also led to adverse reports in newspapers abroad. Some of the Non-European leaders protested against the measure and asserted that the compensation paid for property pulled down was inadequate. But the people actually moved welcomed the change, for they were transferred to well-built cottages in model townships with parks, playing fields, Native shops, etc. The houses had running water and small gardens, and electric lighting is now being provided. In a speech in London in 1957 Mr. Eric Louw said that 'during the past eight years the Government has spent over £40,000,000 on Non-White housing', and added that the policy of providing good houses for Non-Whites would be continued.

Native trade unions were not recognized by the Malan Government, and the claims of the Native workers were dealt with in another way. The Native Labour (Settlement of Disputes) Act of 1953 set up a Central Native Labour Board and provided for the appointment of regional committees and works committees of Natives to further the interests of Native employees. When an industrial council proposes to determine conditions of employment for the purpose of an industrial agreement the Central Native Labour Board and the regional committees must be notified. Strikes, lock-outs and victimization are prohibited under severe penalties—striking by Natives is punishable by a maximum fine of £500 and three years' imprisonment. A Native who does skilled building work in a White area is liable to a fine of £100 and one year's imprisonment.

Native labour bureaux were established to find employment and control Natives in search of work. The Act laid down that Native wages must be paid in cash without deductions and must be paid to the Native personally.

In accordance with his Apartheid policy Malan decided to remove some 38,000 Coloured voters from the Parliamentary roll in the Cape Province and place them on a separate list with power to elect four Europeans to represent them in the House of Assembly. So in 1951 he put before Parliament the Separate Representation of Voters' Bill. It led to what became known as 'the constitutional crisis' which occupied the attention of the law courts, the public and Parliament for five years.

To understand how the issue created a 'constitutional crisis' one must go back to the South Africa Act of 1909, sections 35 and 152 of which laid down that Parliament could not alter the franchise rights of any citizen purely on the ground of his race or colour without the express permission of a two-thirds majority of both Houses of Parliament sitting together.

These were what were called the 'entrenched clauses' in the Union's constitution, and they were not challenged for twenty years. After the passing of the Statute of Westminster however the Appelate Division held in 1937 that the Union Parliament was now the supreme law-making body and was no longer bound by the entrenched clauses in the South Africa Act.

In the light of this ruling Malan put his Separate Representation of Voters' Bill through both Houses of Parliament separately instead of calling a joint sitting and obtaining a two-thirds majority. But in 1952 the Appelate Division declared that the Separate Representation of Voters Act was invalid and null and void because it had not been passed by a two-thirds majority at a joint sitting. It held that the entrenched clauses were still operative despite the judgment given in 1937.

Malan saw that he could not secure a two-thirds majority at a joint sitting, and he determined to get rid of the Coloured vote in the Cape by other methods. He put through Parliament an Act setting up a High Court of Parliament for the express purpose of validating the Separate Representation of Voters Act. The High Court of Parliament—which it was claimed was based on the similar body in England—was duly formed and declared the Separate Representation of Voters Act to be valid.

The issue was again taken to the Appelate Division which declared that the Act setting up the High Court of Parliament was itself invalid and null and void.

Then came the 1953 general election which was fought on the Coloured voters issue. The Nationalists were returned by an increased majority. Malan had privately received promises of support from several members of the Opposition who wished to see the Coloured Voters Bill passed by constitutional means. He believed he could now obtain a two-thirds majority at a joint sitting. He drafted a Bill validating the Separate Representation of Voters Act and twice summoned joint sittings to consider it. On both occasions he failed to secure a two-thirds majority and the Governor-General had to be advised that the Bill had not been passed.

Malan then gave up his attempt to get rid of the Coloured voters. He could have packed the Senate and obtained a two-thirds majority but he decided not to do so. He retired in November, 1954, leaving the Coloured voters in the Cape still on the common roll.

CHAPTER VIII

Two Colour Reports Presented

The implementation of Malan's Apartheid plan did much to clarify the politico-party position on the colour question.

For many years the pronouncements of the two major parties had been nebulous. Both talked vaguely of a 'fair and just' Native policy without revealing any constructive plan for solving the problem of the future relations of Whites and Non-Whites.

The introduction of Apartheid legislation led to closer thinking and the emergence of two well-defined schools of thought.

The National Party, which was almost exclusively Afrikaans, demanded the rigid enforcement of segregation and opposed concessions to the Non-Whites.

The United Party, which contained the majority of the English-speaking section, favoured a more liberal attitude and suggested that attempts should be made to reach a better understanding with the Natives and the Coloureds.

As this dividing line became more marked the reports of two Government Commissions were published, and the rival parties found in one or the other ample justification for the particular plan they put forward.

One, which was known as the Fagan Report, insisted that any colour policy ought to be based on the assumption that there would eventually be a multi-racial society in the Union in which both Whites and Non-Whites must have a permanent place.

The other report, popularly called the Tomlinson Report, demanded the social, residential, industrial and political separation of Whites and Non-Whites and opposed any sharing of authority in the government of the country. The Malan Government accepted it as justifying the Apartheid plan.

In the discussion of the colour problem there have been—and

will be for a long time—constant appeals to one or other of these reports as sanctioning a particular policy, for though they differ in their conclusions they are both based upon a prolonged and careful study of the racial situation in South Africa. The reports of the two commissions are briefly summarized below:

THE FAGAN REPORT

The Fagan Report contains the findings of the Native Laws Commission which was appointed in August 1946 by the Smuts Government to enquire into 'the operation of laws relating to Natives in or near urban areas and the employment of migratory labour and the future policy to be followed in regard thereto'.

The chairman of the Commission was Mr. Justice Henry Allen Fagan, who in later years became the Chief Justice of the Union.

The Commission heard the evidence of a large number of organizations and individuals and visited many urban centres. It examined at great length all the facts and figures relating to the influx of Natives into the towns and found that it was an economic phenomenon which was also affecting other races to an even greater extent than the Bantu. On this movement the Commission found three main trends of thought.

On one wing there were the advocates of a policy that might be called that of total segregation, which envisaged an absolute territorial division so that ultimately there would be a territory in which no Native and another in which no European would be regarded as a permanent inhabitant.

On the other wing the Commission placed those who consider that there should be no racial discrimination at all in law or in administration.

The third view, which the Commission placed between the other two, was that European and Native communities spread all over the country, as is the case today, would continue to exist permanently side by side and must therefore be regarded as permanent; but that there were differences between them which legislation must take into account and which make a measure of separation necessary and advisable.

The Commission noted that the development of the Native Reserves and the purchase of additional ground for them had been the policy of successive South African Governments and said that it believed it to be 'a policy deserving every encouragement and one that does indeed command wide support'.

Studying the existing distribution of the Natives throughout the Union, the Commission found that about sixty per cent of them were in the so-called European areas and only forty per cent in the Native areas. The idea of total segregation therefore assumed that it would be possible to develop and extend the Native areas on a scale sufficient to render them capable of providing a home for more than twice the number of Natives they held today together with the further increase, which would be at an average rate of about two per cent per annum.

Some witnesses, remarked the report, put forward the idea that the Protectorates and other territories outside the Union might be of assistance in providing a home for Natives from the Union. The Commission rejected the idea, saying that 'the stream is flowing into the Union, not out of it, for the simple reason that it flows in the direction of the industries and that the Union is by far the most highly industrialized of all countries in Southern and Central Africa.'

How would the Europeans in South Africa be affected by total segregation? The Commission reported: 'Witnesses have appeared before us who wish to hold out the total withdrawal of the Native from our economic life (that is to say in the European areas) as the ultimate ideal. They concede that it will be a slow process, but they advocate legislation which will promote their ideal by putting obstacles in the way of the employment of Native labourers outside Native areas, and they consider that in the transition period the labour requirements should be satisfied by migratory labour. Others, who concede that they cannot hold out a prospect of the elimination of Native labour from the European industries, advocate migratory labour as a permanent solution. It is however a fact—and must be accepted as such whether we think it desirable or not—that the economic structure of South Africa is based on the one hand on European initiative, organization and technical skill, on the other hand no less on the availability of a few million Native labourers. What would happen if one of these two pillars were knocked down, or even weakened, is pure speculation. We should add that we have seen no sign whatever in the country of a readiness to dispense with Native labour. The best example we can mention in this regard is the farming industry.'

The Commission said that in the rural areas the proportion of

Natives to Europeans was nine to two, yet there was a serious shortage of farm labour. 'Nowhere however,' added the Commissioners, 'did we find the farmer welcoming the movement of Natives from the farms as a step in the right direction, or considering their replacement by European labourers as a practical or desirable alternative. On the contrary all proposals which they put before us were intended to prevail upon Native labourers to remain on, or return to, the farms.'

The Commission described migratory labour as 'a system which in the long run cannot be maintained otherwise than on a limited scale. Under certain circumstances there may in every generation be a number of men and a few women who go forth without their families to work for a while and then return to their homes. If only a relatively small number of young people do that, well and good. But the greater the number who leave—and the more marriageable and married men among them—the greater is the economic, social and moral dislocation in the tribe where the broken families are left behind: and the greater also the disproportion between men and women of their race, with consequent licentiousness, immorality and crime in the places to which they will go. But even if we lull our consciences and risk our safety in the toleration of these evils, it will always be a relatively limited number of people who will offer themselves for migratory labour, and it is inherent in the system itself that they should be at work for only a part of their lives.'

The most important pronouncement in the report of the Fagan Commission was this: 'It should be clear, firstly, that the idea of total segregation is utterly impracticable; secondly, that the movement from country to town has a background of economic necessity—that it may, so one hopes, be guided and regulated and may perhaps also be limited, but that it cannot be stopped or turned back in the opposite direction; and thirdly, that in our urban areas there are not only Native migrant labourers but there is also a settled permanent Native population. These are simply facts which we have to face as such. The old cry 'Send them back' —still so often raised when there is trouble with Natives— therefore no longer offers a solution. A policy based on the proposition that the Natives in the towns are all temporary migrants—or can be kept in the state of temporary migrants—who in the words of the Stallard Commission of 1921 'should only be permitted within municipal areas in so far and for so long as their presence is demanded by the wants of the White population' and 'should depart therefrom when they cease to minister to the needs of the White man' would be a false policy, if for no other reason than because the proposition itself has in the course of time proved to be false. It is however precisely the proposition of the Stallard Commission which lies near the root of many provisions of the legislation relating to Natives in urban areas and has had far-reaching effects in the administration of that legislation throughout the Union. An admission therefore that it is an untenable proposition—and that is an admission which is simply forced upon us by hard facts—make it necessary for us to find a new formula which may serve as a guide in respect of our suggestions for revision of existing legislation.'

The Commission went on to say that from the side of the Natives strong representations were made to them for the removal of all discriminatory laws, for the removal of all restrictions on the movements of Natives, and for direct representation of Natives on town councils. These claims were supported by some European witnesses. The Commission rejected this plea on the ground that the Natives did not form a homogeneous group. There were raw and uncivilized persons among them who needed to be given direction.

Having shown the difficulties that would stand in the way of total segregation, and also of a policy that would allow no racial discrimination, the Commission remarked: 'Only the third policy remains; the policy which recognizes that European and Native communities, scattered throughout the country as they are today, will permanently continue to exist side by side economically intertwined and should therefore be accepted as being permanent and as being part of the same big machine, but that at the same time there are differences between them to which legislation has to pay due regard and which in administrative affairs make necessary and advisable a measure of separation with machinery for consultation on matters of joint concern. We take it, too, that the best development is an evolutionary one and not a revolutionary one . . . We believe that the measures rendered necessary by the new approach should be introduced by way of a gradual change of direction; that we must show respect for existing institutions, for their historical background and for the mentality which is linked with them, and should, where we find it possible, rather build on them than try to overturn them.'

The Commissioners admitted that the enunciation of the policy they had chosen as their guiding principle was vague and general. It meant that the framing of specific proposals might give rise to differences of opinion. Yet they considered this was the only sound way of approaching the problem. 'Providence,' they wrote, 'has ordained that Europeans and Natives shall dwell in South Africa side by side. Conflicts there may be—perhaps less in number if there could have been territorial division, but then their intensity might have been greater and the result more serious as we have seen in Europe in the case of territorially separated nations that differ much less from each other than European and Bantu in South Africa. The relationship, too, will always be fluctuating and changing—for life is dynamic and never stands still—and a cut-and-dried solution is therefore something that cannot be . . . We have simply to take up the task as it is laid upon us; constant adaptation to changing conditions, constant regulation of contacts and smoothing out of difficulties between the races so that all may make their contribution and combine their energies for the progress of South Africa.'

The Commission recommended the formation of Native villages both inside and outside municipal areas, the elimination of those features of the pass system that infuriated the Natives, the delegation of powers to Native boards in local affairs, a centrally organized network of labour bureaux, etc.

In summing up their feelings the Commissioners closed their report by remarking: 'A course of events that can no longer be changed has made South Africa the home of races differing so radically from each other that there can be no question of assimilation, yet economically and territorially so intertwined that they are simply compelled from moment to moment to regulate their contacts, to bridge their differences and to settle their disputes. The Rev. J. H. M. Stofberg, who appeared before us as one of the representatives of the Dutch Reformed Church of the Transvaal, motivated his rejection of the idea of total segregation with the significant words: "For we need them and they need us." Should not we build the best expectation for the future on this simple indisputable fact ?'

The Fagan Commission advocated the continuation and if possible the intensification of the policy of developing the Reserves. This policy should include the combating of soil erosion, supervision over the grazing of cattle, the fencing of camps and the reduction of stock where necessary, improvement of agricultural methods and the establishment of industries where found to be possible.

The Commission, it should be noted, was instructed to enquire into the 'economic and social effects' of the operation of certain laws. It did not, like the later Tomlinson Commission, enquire into the possible political effects of the integration or separation of the European and Non-European races.

THE TOMLINSON REPORT

What is known as the Tomlinson Report is actually the report of the Commission for the Socio-Economic Development of the Bantu Areas Within the Union of South Africa.

It was appointed in 1949 and sat for five years. The chairman was Professor F. R. Tomlinson, of the University of Pretoria, a member of an old Stellenbosch family and a recognized authority on agricultural economics and Bantu affairs.

The Commission made an estimate of the probable numerical differences between the White and Non-White population in years to come.

According to the 1951 census the population of the Union was 12,646,000, composed of 2,643,000 Europeans, 8,575,000 Bantu, 367,000 Asiatics and 1,103,000 Coloured persons. The Bantu population included 650,000 foreign-born Natives who had come into the Union to work and of whom at least one-third must be regarded as permanent residents. The Commission estimated that if the Bantu population had not been strengthened by an influx of Natives from outside the Union the Native population in 1951 would have been almost one million less.

The Commission made two calculations of the probable population of the Union in the year 2000. What it held to be the more likely estimate showed that in that year the total population of the Union would be 31,248,000 which would be divided into 4,588,000 Europeans, 21,361,000 Bantu, 3,917,000 Coloured people and 1,382,000 Asiatics. If however the European population was supplemented by immigration its numerical strength might be at a level between 4,588,000 and 6,150,000.

The Commissioners wrote: 'Future increases in population, in conjunction with further economic development, will result in an increasing urban population, unless this is forestalled by government policy. The anticipated size of this population at the close' of the century will depend upon the assumption upon which the estimates are based. On the basis of present tendencies the numerical share of the Bantu population will gradually increase. If the tempo of urbanization experienced during 1946-1951 is continued to the close of the century, and the projected figure of more than twenty-one million is realized, then more than ten million will be established in the urban areas in the Non-Bantu areas. Moreover if the present absorbent capacity of the Bantu areas, European farms and other rural areas is not raised to such an extent that they can sustain more than the present 6,223,000 Bantu, more than fifteen million of the above mentioned twenty-one million Bantu will be living in the urban areas outside the Bantu areas.'

The report added: 'Unless economic development can be diverted from its present geographical concentration, no other result can be expected than that the relative share of the Bantu in the composition of the urban population will increase. Even if this share should remain constant, their absolute numerical preponderance will increase. It may be anticipated also that the vast majority of these Bantu will be concentrated in the four existing industrial complexes.'

Chapter 25 of the report was headed 'Determination of Policy'. It stated: 'After careful study the Commission has come to the conclusion that the so-called Native question is undoubtedly the most formidable and urgent of South Africa's problems.' The Commission was impressed by the large measure of anxiety and concern that existed in responsible circles—both European and Bantu—as to what the future held in this sphere. But it also noted the ignorance, the absence of any sincere appreciation of the importance and complexity of the problem, the lack of interest and the prejudiced approach evinced in some quarters.

The report continued: 'The Commission wishes to emphasise that a clear and purposeful policy, as well as the logical application and co-ordination of the principles laid down, is absolutely essential if an ultimate condition of affairs unsatisfactory in the highest degree to all sections of the population is to be avoided. Territorial segregation has been the accepted policy of South Africa since the earliest times, and after 1910 was confirmed by the legislation of 1913 and 1936 by means of which some $19\frac{1}{2}$ million morgen of land will eventually be set aside as Bantu territory. The purpose behind these measures was undoubtedly to create a national home

for the Bantu, while at the same time limiting their rights in the
non-Bantu areas . . . Our legislative policy therefore attempts to
bring about territorial separation—or a large measure of it—
and thus also territorial separateness as regards political and social
development. The policy has not however been fully implemented
or followed to its logical conclusion. Bantu are leaving the Reserves
in ever greater numbers to settle permanently in the non-Bantu
areas. The following factors are responsible for this situation:

1. The undeveloped and backward state of the Bantu areas;
2. The slow rate of progress in the purchase of land under
   the 1936 Act;
3. The process of economic integration that has taken place
   on such a large scale during the past decade as the result
   of a number of factors; and
4. The slow and half-hearted manner in which administrative
   powers were conferred on the Bantu in the Bantu areas.
   Seen from the point of view of geographical distribution of
   population, the policy has however shown positive results
   in the sense that the Bantu areas are today the domicile of
   slightly more than half of the Union-born Bantu.'

The Commission found that at whatever speed, and in whatever
manner, the evolutionary process of integration and equalization
between European and Bantu might take place, there could be
no doubt as to the ultimate outcome in the political sphere,
namely, that the control of political power would pass into the
hands of the Bantu. It remarked however that even more important
was the consideration that over the past three hundred years the
European population of the Union had developed into an autonomous and complete national organism and had further preserved
its character as a biological (racial) entity. There were not the
slightest grounds for believing that the European population,
either now or in the future, would be willing to sacrifice its character as a national entity and as a European racial group. The
combination of these two factors made the position and struggle
of the European people in South Africa unique in the world. That
the European people would not be prepared willingly to sacrifice
their right of existence as a separate national and racial entity
must be accepted as the dominant fact in the South African
situation.

The Commission insisted that the Europeans were determined to keep their political destiny in their own hands; while among the Bantu there was a growing desire to take part in the government of the country. It was clear that a continuation of the policy of integration 'would intensify racial friction and animosity, and that the only alternative is to promote the establishment of separate communities in their own separate territories where each will have the fullest opportunity of self-expression and development.'

Closer examination of the possibilities of a 'middle-of-the-road' policy and a *laissez-faire* policy led the Commission to conclude that both of these alternatives must be discarded as offering no hope of a solution of the problem. The importance of the economic considerations could not be under-rated; but the economic aspect was only one facet of the problem, and the decision rested with the people themselves as to which factor or group of factors was to be regarded as paramount. If the European population decided for economic reasons to continue the process of integration it would have to accept the political and social consequences of such action; if on the other hand it considered that political and social considerations were of primary importance it must be prepared to restrict and replace the process of integration. For the Bantu population the choice was no less momentous; it had to decide whether it wished to form part of a community in which it would for obvious reasons be under constant restraint, or whether it desired to adopt a fuller life as a separate national entity in its own territory.

'The argument is sometimes used,' remarked the Commission, 'that the Bantu areas are not large enough, or do not possess the required potential for development to make a policy of separate development a practical proposition. It appears in the light of the knowledge we now possess that the Bantu areas properly developed would be capable of carrying a population equal to that of the present population of the Union and of providing them with a reasonable standard of living. The development of industries in the so-called border areas would help to accommodate an even larger Bantu population in the Bantu areas . . . The Commission is of opinion that the High Commission Territories should be incorporated in the Union as soon as possible. The implementation of the policy of separate development would have to be effected, as far as the foreseeable future is concerned, within the framework of the consolidated Bantu areas of the Union, those of South West Africa and the High Commission Territories. Circumstances necessitate that a clear and unequivocal choice be made, and the obvious way out of the dilemma is to proceed with large-scale sustained development of the Bantu areas.'

The Commission found that the policy of separate development was a prerequisite for the sound development of the Bantu communities, and in particular would bring—

(1) their own inalienable territory;
(2) the creation of opportunities for individual and communal development;
(3) the opportunity to take charge of their own affairs; and
(4) full opportunity for economic development, *inter alia*, in the direction of (a) greater economic diversification, (b) creation of a entrepreneurial class, (c) opportunities for entering the professions and semi-skilled and skilled employment, (d) the provision of extensive social services and security, and (e) the building up of a sound social order.

The Commission declared: 'The policy of separate development is the only means by which the Europeans can ensure their future unfettered existence by which increasing race tensions and clashes can be avoided, and by means of which the Europeans will be able fully to meet their responsibilities as guardians of the Bantu population. The European population should therefore be willing to take the necessary steps to put this policy into effect.'

The Commissioners felt that they were justified in commenting on the question of general policy because: (1) the problem was not one that could be dealt with piecemeal; (2) their conclusions provide the most urgent reason why the European population should be willing to grant the extensive financial, technical and other assistance required for the proper development of the Bantu areas, and why the co-operation of the Bantu people could be expected in this development; (3) the preservation and continuation of the Reserves as Bantu areas can only be entertained and justified on the grounds of these considerations of principle.

The Commission asked: 'What area would be available for the separate development of the Bantu tribes?' In reply it insisted that the consolidation of the 260 separate scattered Native Reserves was essential. Save for a few blocks the Bantu areas were so scattered that they formed no foundation for common growth. Even if the potentiality of the existing fragmentary areas was such that it could provide the entire Bantu population with a means of living, this fragmentation could result in nothing else than a supplementary growth attached to the European community.

The Commission pointed out that the Bantu 'heartlands', the Transkei, Basutoland, Zululand, Swaziland, Sekkukhuneland, Vendaland and Bechuanaland, had always been preserved by the Europeans. Although the High Commission Territories were artificially excluded from the Union in 1910, these Territories remained the 'heartlands' of the Bantu inside the Territories as well as outside the Territories in the Union. In 1913 and again in 1936 the legislators of the Union very clearly set aside the Bantu areas taking into account the cultural-historical bonds of the Bantu, including those of the three High Commission Territories.

The Commission recommended the consolidation of the Bantu areas into seven blocks which could be systematically constructed around the seven historico-logical nuclei or 'heartlands'. After suggesting ways of forming and controlling the seven blocks of Native Territory, the Commission remarked: 'The coming into being of the seven Bantu Areas each surrounding a "heartland" will mean that the British South Africa of 1902, which covered 765,915 square miles, will be about evenly divided between Europeans and Bantu. 275,000 square miles of Bechuanaland, 6,705 square miles of Swaziland, 11,716 square miles of Basutoland, and approximately 65,000 square miles of the Union, will then be set aside for exclusive utilization by Bantu. The total extent of the Bantu areas will then be 358,421 square miles, or approximately 47 per cent of the former British South Africa. In arriving at this estimate the size of the Bantu areas of the Union was placed at 19,611,468 morgen, or about 65,000 square miles, while the whole of Swaziland, and not only the Bantu portion, was included in the calculation.'

The Commission reported in detail and at great length on the possible economic development of the Bantu areas, dealing with farming, irrigation, forestry, mining, sugar-cane growing and secondary industries. It worked out elaborate schemes for administration, health services, education, etc., with estimates of the cost of the various services.

It arrived at the conclusion that the existing system of land tenure in the Bantu areas did not provide security of tenure or an adequate means of existence. It recommended that the present exclusively agricultural population of these areas should be divided into an agricultural class, with each farmer getting sufficient ground for an economic farm, and an urban class which would have to find means of existence in industry, the professions, etc. Title deeds to both farming and urban land in the Bantu areas should be granted to the Bantu who purchased such land. This new form of ownership should replace all present forms of tenure.

The Commission insisted that there must be no delay in taking practical steps for implementing the proposals made. It said: 'The concentration of economic development in a few regions, especially as regards secondary industry, continues unabated; this concentration demands continual expansion of the services, which in turn attracts more undertakings and increased population. This aggravates the backward position of the Bantu areas and hinders the initiation of development in those areas . . . At present tempo the Bantu population of the existing "White" urban areas is increasing by about 85,000 a year. A continuance of this present intensity of urbanization will ensure a Bantu population of ten and a quarter million in these areas by the end of the century, and the limited capacity of agriculture to accommodate increasing numbers may even raise this figure.'

The Commission declared: 'If a programme such as the one outlined is not tackled and present conditions continue, it cannot be expected that the Bantu areas will ever contain many more people than are residing there at the present stage. The increase in population there will simply "overflow" to other parts of the country. In that case by the close of the century the European areas will probably accommodate no less than three-quarters of the Bantu population.'

On the basis of the inherent potential of the Bantu areas the Commission's development programme envisaged the attainment of a total population of ten millions in the Bantu areas within a period of 25–30 years. Of this number it was estimated that eight millions would be dependent for their existence on activities within the Bantu areas and two million on activities in the European sector. If the Bantu areas were not developed, the European sector would probably have to accommodate a Bantu population of about seventeen millions at the close of the century. It was estimated that the total requirements for development in the first ten years would cost £104,486,000.

In its recommendations the Commission again stressed its main conclusion. It said: 'The present tendency towards integration in

South Africa is undoubtedly resulting in the two groups becoming interwoven to an increasing degree. The lesson of history is that if it takes place in an evolutionary manner such intertwining of two groups eventually leads to the rise of a unified community . . . The Commission is convinced that in South Africa there is little hope of evolutionary development in the direction outlined. The dilemma which confronts the population of South Africa as a result of the process of integration is evident. On the European side there is an unbreakable will to maintain their identity in a national and biological sense; on the side of the Bantu population there is to an increasing extent the conviction that they are entitled to enjoy the fruits of integration *inter alia* by demanding progressively an increasing say in the administration of the country as a whole. A further aspect of the dilemma is that if the process of integration is to be altered a re-orientation of the economic structure of the country may become necessary in the long run.

'The conclusion arrived at by the Commission is that circumstances demand a speedy, definite and unambiguous decision. The Commission is convinced that the separate development of the European and Bantu communities should be striven for as the only direction in which racial conflict may possibly be eliminated and racial harmony possibly be maintained. The only obvious way out of the dilemma lies in the sustained development of the Bantu areas on a large scale. This is the germinal point in the presence of separate development of European and Bantu. The Commission is convinced that there is no midway between the two poles of ultimate total integration and ultimate separate development of the two groups.'

The Commission concluded its report with these words: 'It is the conviction of the Commission that the development programme must be tackled in the spirit of an act of faith, in the same manner in which many other great undertakings in the Union have already been launched as acts of faith at times when the chances of success were at their minimum or were totally denied by some people. If it is permissible for the Commission to draw a comparison, it would like to point out that the task set in its report cannot be described as impossible, indeed not even as exceptionally difficult, when it is compared with the task of reconstructing the war-devastated countries after 1945. And these countries succeeded in their task. The choice is clear: either its *challenge* must be accepted or the inevitable *consequences* of the integration of the

Bantu and European populations into a common society must be endured.'

Dr. Bisschop, a member of the Commission, tabled a minority report in which he reviewed the three policies he called integration, the 'halfway' or 'middle of the road' idea, and the segregation plan. The two former could not be tested out in practice because to do so it would be necessary to remove the present discriminatory regulations and usages, and once these had been removed it would not be possible to re-introduce them. He went on: 'The "segregation" formula however can be tested out in practice without necessarily affecting the Europeans or Bantu adversely. It is therefore the duty of the Europeans towards themselves, the Bantu and posterity, to investigate fully the potentialities of the Bantu areas, to determine the number of Bantu that can be accommodated permanently in the Bantu areas under conditions which will allow of the attainment of their legitimate aspirations, and to draw up plans for the efficient exploitation of the Bantu areas for—and as far as possible by—the Bantu themselves . . . The practicability of the "segregation" formula must be fully investigated and tested out. If in due course it is found unpractical, and I greatly fear it will be found to be so, progressive integration with its economic and political consequences will have to be accepted.'

The Strijdom Government issued a White Paper on the Tomlinson Report. It stated: 'The Government welcomes the unequivocal rejection of the policy of integration and of any theories of a possible middle course, as well as the justification by the Commission of the Government's policy of Apartheid (Separate Development) as gradually but purposefully applied. It also welcomes the endorsement of the Government's repeatedly expressed standpoint that sufficiently rapid progress will have been made and further advancement of the process of separation guaranteed, in other words that security would be assured for White civilization, and opportunities created for both racial groups in all spheres, if after a period of fifty years an approximately equal proportion of Whites and Bantu has been reached in European territory.'

The White Paper surveyed the recommendations of the Commission in detail. The Government accepted most of the principles underlying the recommendations but rejected some of the proposals for carrying them out. It was not prepared to do away with the tribal tenure of rural land and to substitute individual tenure based on purchase, nor did it propose to 'give preference to individual acquisition of land above tribal and Trust purchases in the released areas'. On the recommendations regarding irrigation, the checking of soil erosion, the cultivation of fibre, and sugar-cane, forestry and so on, the Government agreed with the principles, which were already being carried out, but did not accept the need for setting up new bodies to undertake the work.

The Government accepted the policy that Bantu enterprise unimpeded by European competition should be enabled to develop its own industries—with or without assistance—inside the Bantu areas, but could not agree that private European industrialists should be permitted to go into those areas. It stated that it regarded the development of industries owned by Europeans, but requiring large numbers of Bantu labourers, in suitable European areas near Bantu territory 'as of the utmost importance for the sound socio-economic development of the Bantu areas' and intended to take the necessary steps to create the desired conditions for attracting industries to such areas.

On the suggested consolidation of the Bantu areas, the Government agreed broadly with the principle but remarked: 'Since large portions of the released areas must still be acquired under the Native Trust and Land Act of 1936 it is however unrealistic to indicate at present vague boundaries on maps which involve European land the acquisition of which cannot possibly now be considered. Future Governments may have reason to return to such theories. At the present moment this is not a practical issue.'

In July 1956 a congress, summoned by the South African Bureau of Racial Affairs, the Federated Dutch Reformed Churches and the Federation of Afrikaans Cultural Societies, met at Bloemfontein and was attended by eight hundred delegates representing 540 organizations. One of the resolutions adopted by the congress declared that 'there is no possibility of the peaceful evolutionary development of White and Bantu in South Africa into an integrated society', and that the policy of integration 'can only lead to the destruction of one or both of the groups'. The congress accepted the broad principles of the Tomlinson Report and expressed its appreciation to the Government for the serious way in which it was tackling the racial problems of the country.

Professor Tomlinson spoke at the meeting and insisted that the total support of the population of South Africa for this development programme was vitally necessary. 'It is,' he said, 'a matter of life or death. May the present generation be big enough to accept this challenge. The decision rests with them, for the next ten or fifteen years will be decisive. There is no other choice.' He said that if the Reserves were not developed, he was absolutely sure that they would be saddled with nineteen million Natives in urban areas to about five and a half million Whites. An isolated four million Bantu would also eke out a miserable existence in the Bantu areas.

What the majority of the Non-White organizations thought of the Tomlinson Report was shown at a conference held at Bloemfontein in October 1955, sponsored by the Inter-denominational African Ministers' Federation and presided over by Chief A. J. Luthuli, the president of the African National Congress. Some four hundred delegates attended the conference, which it was claimed represented all shades of Native opinion.

Professor Z. K. Matthews, the vice-president of the African National Congress, told the conference that it was now clear that only the endeavours of the Bantu themselves could gain independence for them. The life of the Black man in South Africa consisted of one crisis after another. The policy of White mastery showed no signs of being lifted. The Apartheid tempo was being hastened and merciless attempts were being made to achieve the goal while completely ignoring the consequences of that policy.

Professor Matthews added that the Nationalist accentuation of White domination had not yet led the Africans into a counter-demand for Black *baasskap*. 'We are not opposed,' he went on, 'to the White man or anyone else claiming for themselves in the land in which they have made their home all the fundamental rights to which as human beings they are entitled. What we cannot concede is that this is a claim of which the White man has the monopoly.'

The conference devoted three days to studying the Tomlinson Report. It rejected the recommendations of the Commission *in toto*. Its rejection was based upon three main objections:

(1) The Tomlinson Report acknowledged that 'a solution of this problem will only have been achieved when a satisfactory arrangement in regard to the political aspect is arrived at', but the conference found that 'there was nothing in the Report remotely resembling a satisfactory arrangement with regard to the political aspect'.

(2) The conference could not accept the Commission's view that there were only two alternatives for South Africa—'complete integration' or 'complete segregation'. It maintained that 'a proper reading of the South African situation calls for co-operation and interdependence between the various races comprising the South African nation and denies that this arrangement would constitute a threat to the survival of the White man in South Africa'.

(3) The conference felt that the net result of the implementation of the Tomlinson Report would be 'a continuation of the *status quo* and indeed an aggravation of the worst evils of the present system including their extension to the Protectorates'.

Viewing the Report against the background of the Government's attitude to it, the conference declared: 'This conference notes that the Government itself in its White Paper on the Report has rejected some of the principal and most significant recommendations of the Commission and has thus undermined the goals which it sets out to achieve. Thus the claim that the Government is moving in the direction of these goals emerges as a hollow political bluff'.

Reviewing some of the details of the Tomlinson Report the conference advanced objections that may be summarized thus:

Economic: The conference could find no justification for the view that the development of the Native Reserves should be linked with Apartheid. It agreed that the rehabilitation of the Reserves was sound policy for the general good of the country. But it could not accept any plan for the separate development of the Reserves 'coupled with deprivation of basic and economic rights and opportunities in the rest of the country designed for the implementation of the ideology of Apartheid'.

Civil Rights: The conference challenged the Commission's statement that in regard to their 'wider civil rights' Africans were 'substantially in no worse position than other sections of the population'. The conference said that Africans suffered from glaring inequalities and civil disabilities—a policy which seriously threatened orderly government and the foundations of South Africa as a viable State.

Separate Areas: The conference rejected the postulate that Africans had less claim to certain parts of South Africa than Europeans; they were the indigenous people of the country; there was no part of the country to the development of which they had not made their full contribution; the concept of 'national homes' for the Africans facilitated the exploitation and economic strangulation of the Africans and perpetuated White domination.

The conference appealed to all national organizations to mobilize all people, irrespective of race, colour or creed, to form a united front against Apartheid, and to the Christian churches to take 'a clear and unequivocal stand in defence of Christian and human values being trampled underfoot in the name of Apartheid'. It reiterated the demand of the African peoples for the abolition of discriminatory laws and the extension of full citizenship rights to all 'which alone would guarantee peaceful and harmonious relations between Black and White'.

CHAPTER IX

Strijdom insists upon "Baasskap"

Dr. D. F. Malan resigned his position as Prime Minister on November 30, 1954, and retired from public life.

The National Party caucus chose Johannes Gerhardus Strijdom as its new leader, and the Governor-General asked him to form a government.

With the going of Malan there went the political atmosphere of the older generation. Although 'the Doctor' had proclaimed the policy called Apartheid, he had been brought up in the milder atmosphere of the old Cape Colony.

Strijdom was the leader of the extreme wing of the Transvaal Nationalists who stood for a more rigid attitude on the colour question. He was uncompromising in his views and never hesitated to proclaim them in unmistakeable language. His admirers used to say: 'You know where you are with Hans Strijdom.'

The Strijdom Government met Parliament for the first time in January 1955, and in that and subsequent sessions it showed that it was determined to beat down all opposition to the strict enforcement of the separation policy.

When Strijdom became Prime Minister he found that the Coloured voters in the Cape were still on the common roll. For four years the Malan administration had tried to remove them but could never get the two-thirds majority in the joint sitting which the Appeal Court ruled was essential for the validity of any Act making the change.

Strijdom resolved to succeed where his predecessor had failed. He abandoned the idea of obtaining a two-thirds majority in Parliament with the support of dissident members of the United Party. First, he enlarged the Appellate Division of the Supreme Court by adding five more judges and laying down that in a case attacking the validity of an Act of Parliament there must be a quorum of eleven judges. Next he increased the membership of the Senate from 48 to 89 in such a way that 77 of the members would be Nationalists. Then at a joint sitting the Government would be able to command 171 votes, or five more than was necessary to obtain a two-thirds majority at a joint sitting.

Despite angry protests from the Opposition, the Bills making these changes were passed; and then the Government summoned a joint sitting and placed before it the South Africa Act Amendment Bill which validated the Separate Representation of Voters Act of 1951. Thanks to the packed Senate the Government secured 173 votes to 68—seven more than the essential two-thirds majority.

Again the measure was taken to the Appeal Court, and at last, in October 1955, a bench of eleven judges, by a majority of ten to one, held that the Separate Representation of Voters Act was now valid. Consequently some thirty thousand Coloured men in the Cape lost the right to vote at a Parliamentary election.

Strijdom was determined to exclude Non-Whites from the Parliamentary polling booths because he held that once they were allowed to enter them they would in the end form the majority of the electors. With characteristic outspokenness he did not hesitate to explain exactly why he would give Non-Whites no share in the government of the country. In Parliament in April 1955 he defended his colour policy with almost brutal frankness. He said that there was only one way in which the White man could maintain his leadership of the Non-Europeans and that was by domination.

'Call it paramountcy, *baasskap* or what you will,' he went on, 'it is still domination. I am being as blunt as I can. I am making no excuses. Either the White man dominates or the Black man takes over. I say that the Non-European will not accept leadership —if he has a choice. The only way the Europeans can maintain supremacy is by domination . . . And the only way they can maintain domination is by withholding the vote from the Non-Europeans. If it were not for that we would not be here in Parliament today. It is because the voting power is in the hands of the White man that the White man is able to govern South Africa today. Under the existing law it is not possible for the Natives, through merit or any other means, to get the government into their hands. The government of the country is in the hands of the White

man as the result of the franchise laws, and for that reason the
White man is *baas* in South Africa . . . To suggest that the White
man can maintain leadership purely on the grounds of his greater
competency is unrealistic. The greater competency of the White
man can never weigh against numbers if Natives and Europeans
enjoy equal voting rights.'

The United Party rejected the policy of *baasskap* and insisted
that the Non-Europeans must be given some share in the government of the country. At the same time they denied that the party
stood for equality.

While stressing the necessity for White supremacy, Strijdom
strove to persuade the Non-Europeans that his Apartheid policy
was in their own interests, and that he desired to place them under
happier conditions.

In a speech in December 1955, he said that South Africa's
traditional policy of separating the White and Non-White races in
all spheres of public life must be so applied as to prove that there
was no hostility towards the Non-Whites and no intention of
oppressing them. For many years successive Governments in the
Union had spent proportionately more on uplifting and aiding its
Non-White people than any other White government in Africa
or elsewhere. This fact, as it became better understood by the
Non-Whites, was contributing greatly towards counteracting
poisonous propaganda spread among the Non-Whites by the
opponents of South Africa. Owing to this propaganda the task of
the Government was exceedingly difficult.

He went on: 'In our actions towards the Non-Whites in the
application of our traditional policy of separation we shall have to
act in such a way as to give proof that we are not hostile towards
the Non-Whites; that separation is in the interests of both colour
groups; and that with this policy clashes and friction are eliminated
and co-existence, but not integration, is assured.'

To the head of an American Press agency Strijdom explained
the Apartheid policy by saying that the only way to be fair to the
Black man was to allow him 'slowly, as he develops, to obtain
political and other rights in his own areas under the White man's
guidance . . . Ultimately it is part of the Apartheid policy that
educated Natives should be doctors, chemists, builders, traders,
civil servants, policemen and so forth in their own areas so that
there can be no question of frustrating them or preventing them
from rising to the top among their own people. In other words

we want the Bantu to look on his Native Reserve as his homeland, to develop a love for it and to accept the policy that in his part of the country he will be protected and given an opportunity to practice all the occupations which are reserved to the White man in his area. If a policy of this kind is not carried out you must allow him all these privileges in the White man's area; and if you do that it is a matter of simple arithmetic that in a few decades the White man will be completely submerged.'

The supporters of the African National Congress were not impressed by promises of a better life in the Native Reserves. Although the defiance campaign had had to be abandoned, it was noticed that at Bantu gatherings there was a more general singing of national songs such as 'Lord Bless Africa' and 'Let Africa Return', which have a strong emotional appeal. There was also a wider use of the greeting of the liberation or resistance movement which takes the form of a long-drawn call of 'Africa' while the right fist is clenched with the thumb held erect and the arm moved towards the shoulder.

A Congress of the People was then summoned to meet at Kliptown, near Johannesburg, on June 26, 1955. It was attended by some three thousand delegates from the African National Congress, the Indian Congress, the Coloured Peoples Organization and the Congress Democrats.

The police were present in considerable numbers during the meeting of the Congress of the People and on the second day cleared the hall and prevented further proceedings.

Before the Congress was broken up it had however adopted 'The Freedom Charter' which was in these terms:

'We, the people of South Africa, declare for all our country and the world to know

that South Africa belongs to all who live in it, Black and White, and that no Government can justly claim authority unless it is based on the will of all the people;

that our people have been robbed of their birthright to land, liberty and peace by a form of government founded on injustice and inequality;

that our country will never be prosperous or free until all our people live in brotherhood, enjoying equal rights and opportunities;

that only a democratic State based on the will of all the

people can secure to all their birthright without distinction of colour, race, sex or belief;

'And therefore we, the people of South Africa, Black and White together—equals, countrymen and brothers—adopt this Freedom Charter. And we pledge ourselves to strive together, sparing neither strength nor courage, until the democratic changes here set out have been won.

'Every man and woman shall have the right to vote for, and to stand as a candidate for, all bodies that make laws. All people shall be entitled to take part in the administration of the country. The rights of the people shall be the same, regardless of race, colour or sex.

'All bodies of minority rule, boards, councils and authorities, shall be replaced by democratic organs of self-government.

'There shall be equal status in the bodies of the State, in the courts and the schools for all national groups and races. All people shall have equal right to use their own languages and to develop their own folk culture and customs.

'All national groups shall be protected by law against insults to their race and national pride; the preaching and practice of national race or colour discrimination and contempt shall be a punishable offence. All Apartheid laws shall be set aside.

'The national wealth of our country, the heritage of all South Africans, shall be restored to the people. The mineral wealth beneath the soil, the banks and monopoly industry shall be transferred to the ownership of the people as a whole. All other industry and trade shall be controlled to assist the well-being of the people. All people shall have equal rights to trade where they choose, to manufacture, and to enter all trades, crafts and professions.

'Restriction of land ownership on a racial basis shall be ended, and all land re-divided amongst those who work it, to banish famine and land hunger. The State shall help the peasants with implements, seed, tractors and dams to save the soil and assist the tillers. Freedom of movement shall be guaranteed to all who work on the land. All shall have the right to occupy land wherever they choose. People shall not be robbed of their cattle, and forced labour and farm prisons shall be abolished.

'No one shall be imprisoned, deported or restricted without a fair trial. No one shall be condemned by order of any Government official. The courts shall be representative of all the people. Imprisonment shall be only for serious crimes against the people, and shall aim at re-education and not vengeance. The police force and the army shall be open to all on an equal basis and shall be the helpers and protectors of the people. All laws which discriminate on grounds of race, colour or belief shall be repealed.

'The law shall guarantee to all their right to speak, to organize, to meet together, to publish, to preach, to worship and to educate their children. The privacy of the house from police raids shall be protected by law. All shall be free to travel without restriction from countryside to town, from province to province, and from South Africa abroad. Pass laws, permits and all other laws restricting these freedoms shall be abolished.

'All who work shall be free to form trade unions, to elect their officers and to make wage arrangements with their employers. The State shall recognize the right and duty of all to work and to draw full unemployment benefits. Men and women of all races shall receive equal pay for equal work. There shall be a forty-hour working week, a national minimum wage, paid annual leave, and sick leave for all workers, and maternity leave on full pay for all working mothers. Miners, domestic workers, farm workers and civil servants shall have the same rights as all others who work. Child labour, compound labour, the tot system and contract labour shall be abolished.

'The Government shall discover, develop and encourage national talent for the enhancement of our cultural life. All the cultural treasures of mankind shall be open to all by free exchange of books, ideas and contact with other lands. The aim of education shall be to teach the youth to love their people and their culture, to honour human brotherhood, liberty and peace. Education shall be free, compulsory, universal and equal for all children. Higher education and technical training shall be open to all by means of State allowances and scholarships awarded on the basis of merit. Adult illiteracy shall be ended by a mass education plan. Teachers shall have all the rights of other citizens. The colour bar in cultural life, in sport and in education shall be abolished.

'All people shall have the right to live where they choose, to be decently housed and to bring up their families in comfort and security. Unused housing space to be made available to the people. Rents and prices shall be lowered, food shall be plentiful and no one shall go hungry.

'A preventive health scheme shall be run by the State. Free medical care and hospitalization shall be provided for all with special care for mothers and young children. Slums shall be abolished and new suburbs built where all have transport, roads, lighting, playing fields, creches and social centres. The aged, the orphans, the disabled and the sick shall be cared for by the State. Leisure and recreation shall be the right of all. Fenced ghettos and locations shall be abolished and laws that break up families shall be repealed.

'South Africa shall be a fully independent State which respects the rights and sovereignity of all nations. South Africa shall strive to maintain world peace and the settlement of international disputes by negotiation—not war. Peace and friendship among all our people shall be secured by upholding the equal rights, opportunities and status of all. The people of the Protectorates—Basutoland, Bechuanaland and Swaziland—shall be free to decide for themselves their own future. The right of all the people of Africa to independence and self-government shall be recognized and shall be the basis of close co-operation.

'Let all who love their people and their country now say, as we say here

THESE FREEDOMS WE WILL FIGHT FOR SIDE BY SIDE THROUGHOUT OUR LIVES UNTIL WE HAVE WON OUR LIBERTY.'

The Charter of Freedom was freely quoted by the prosecution in the later treason trials as evidence that the defendants were influenced by communistic ideas and had plotted to overthrow the existing State and replace it by a communistic form of government.

Early in 1956 the Government closed the two Russian consulates in the Union on the ground that the members of the staffs had 'cultivated and maintained contact with subversive elements in the Union, particularly among the Bantu and Indian population, and that the consulates had served as a channel of communication between such elements and the authorities of Soviet Russia'. Several members of the Government alluded in public speeches to the danger of subversive activities in the country and the necessity for guarding against them.

Suddenly, before daybreak on December 5, 1956, members of the Special Branch of the police entered the homes of some one hundred and fifty people in different parts of the country and arrested 156 individuals on a charge of high treason—for which the penalty is death. Among them were several Europeans, including one of the Native representatives in Parliament and two former members of the Cape Provincial Council. Clergymen, doctors, lawyers, journalists and teachers were among the prisoners who were taken to the Fort, the central prison in Johannesburg. For three days they were only allowed to see their lawyers, and their letters were censored and bail was refused. Later however bail was accepted.

As there was no court large enough for a mass trial the Drill Hall in Johannesburg was fitted up as a court. The preparatory examination began on December 19 and the court adjourned in order to put in microphones and arrange for interpreters to be available. The prisoners had been placed in a huge dock with wire netting five feet high round much of it, giving the appearance of a vast cage. On the second day all the counsel for the defence threatened to walk out unless the wire was removed. The front and sides of the cage were then taken down and replaced by railings.

Large crowds of Natives assembled outside the court, although there was only accommodation inside for two hundred spectators. Stones were thrown at the police outside the hall and there were baton charges and finally the police opened fire. Two Europeans were reported to have received bullet wounds and twenty Natives were taken to hospital. There were complaints that the police arrested three Press photographers and destroyed the pictures they had taken of the rioting. Subsequently some five hundred police cordoned off the area around the court.

The Crown Prosecutor stated that the basis of the charge of high treason would be incitement and preparation for the overthrowing of the existing State by revolutionary methods involving violence and the establishment of a so-called people's democracy on the basis of the Eastern European Communist satellite States and China.

The preliminary examination went on for months and ten thousand documents were put in and scores of detectives gave evidence.

In September 1957 the court adjourned until the following year, and in the interval the Attorney-General withdrew the charges against all but twenty-nine of the accused, who were committed for trial before three judges sitting in a special court. Suddenly at the end of March 1961 the three judges acquitted all the accused. They held that there was no evidence that the African National Congress had planned to overthrow the existing form of government by violence. Despite this judgment the Government continued to proclaim the Congress an illegal body. The case aroused much interest overseas, and a fund was opened in England to pay for the defence of the accused and assist those who had been deprived of their livelihood by having to appear in court year after year, and about £173,000 was raised. It was estimated that the case cost the State £350,000. The judgment was received with great rejoicing by the Non-Whites and was welcomed abroad as evidence of the impartiality of the courts in South Africa.

While the treason trial dragged on, the Strijdom Government, convinced that the future of the White race could only be safeguarded by a sustained policy of separation, drafted measures to restrict the existing contacts between White and Non-White and to encourage the Bantu to establish their own institutions.

In 1956 the Minister of Labour (Senator J. de Klerk) put through Parliament the Industrial Conciliation Act which was based on the principle of separation. It encouraged the formation of racially separate trade unions, for the members of one race in a trade union with a mixed racial membership were entitled to set up a separate trade union for their own race group provided that fifty per cent of the members of that particular group favoured such a change. Another clause made provision for the reservation of certain categories of work for members of a particular race group if it proved necessary to protect the interests of that race group. Thus certain classes of work could be reserved for Whites. Bantu trade unions were not prohibited but they were not to be given official recognition by way of registration. It was argued that the Bantu were sufficiently protected by the operation of the existing Wage Boards.

In a speech to industrialists, Strijdom said that the most fundamental issue facing the Whites in South Africa was the preservation of the White race and Western civilization. It was therefore vital that the right choice should be made between integration, with its inevitable result of destruction for the White man, or separate development. Industrialists in South Africa could no longer defer making the choice. While fairness and justice should be meted out to the Non-European nothing should be done that would jeopardize the White man's survival, safety and supremacy.

'We have reached the cross-road,' he continued, 'the choice of the right course now could lead to safety and salvation. The adoption of the wrong course must inevitably lead to our destruction within the next few generations—whatever temporary material advantage the present and possibly the next generation might derive from the adoption of such a course. Together with the rest of the country you, too, as industrialists will have to make your choice—now or in the near future.'

Industrial expansion in the Union had led to the employment of a larger number of Whites; yet the percentage of Europeans engaged in secondary industry steadily declined. It was found that in the engineering trade 95 per cent of the manufacturing divisions in the industry were manned by Bantu while the percentage of skilled artisans had dropped to a mere thirteen per cent of the total labour force. In the motor trade the ratio of White to Non-White directly employed in the assembly of motor vehicles fell from 82 per cent to 54 per cent between the years 1949 and 1954. In the commercial distributive trade the percentage of Whites employed as motor vehicle drivers dropped from 57 per cent in 1937 to 20 per cent in 1951.

The Strijdom Government investigated numerous industries with the idea of reserving certain classes of work for Whites and it had the support of the majority of the members of the trade unions who believed that there must be protection against the use of Non-White workers at cheap rates of pay; otherwise their own hard-won standards would be destroyed. Naturally the Non-White organizations opposed this policy. The employers on the whole were against it on the ground that it would send up production costs and make it more difficult for them to meet competition from countries in which the factory output per worker was often far greater than in South Africa. Mr. B. J. Schoeman, the Minister of Transport, said: 'The statutory colour bar as well as the conventional colour bar are in conflict with economic laws. The question however is this: What is our first consideration? Is it to maintain economic laws or is it to ensure the continued existence of the European race in this country?'

In 1957 the Government introduced the Separate University Education Bill. It provided for the establishment of university colleges for the Bantu and other Non-White groups. The colleges would be controlled by the Government, which would appoint the principal, council and senate of each college. The Minister

responsible for the control of a particular college would have the
right to refuse entrance to any particular student of the race group
concerned if he considered that such refusal would be in the
interests of the college. The staff of the colleges would be the
employees of the Government and would be subject to the normal
disciplinary control imposed in other teaching institutions, but in
addition they would not be permitted to propagate ideas which
were calculated to cause or promote antagonism amongst any
section of the population against any other section or which were
prejudicial to the administration, discipline or efficiency of any
university college, Government department or other public
institution. This limitation also applied to adverse comments on a
Government department if such comment was publicly voiced.

Other clauses provided for the gradual limitation of Non-White
attendance at White universities. Non-Whites undergoing courses
at White universities would be able to complete them; but after a
certain date the attendance of Non-Whites at White universities
would require Ministerial permission and ultimately complete
separation would be enforced. The Bantu university colleges
would fall under the Department of Native Affairs, which also
administered Bantu school education, while the proposed Coloured
and Indian colleges and also the Non-White Medical School
would fall under the Department of Education, Arts and Science.
The Fort Hare University College and the Non-White Medical
School of the University of Natal would be placed under the
control of the Government.

The Government scheme envisaged the setting up of five
university colleges and a medical school for Non-Whites. Three
of the colleges would provide for the three main ethnic Bantu
groups—Sotho, Zulu and Xhosa—and one would be for Coloureds
and one for Indians. The University of South Africa would lay
down the curricula to be followed in the various courses provided
at each college, and the University would also be the examining
body for all the colleges. University authorities were prohibited
from admitting racially disqualified students.

The Government's proposals were immediately and widely
criticized. The United Party opposed even the introduction of the
Bill into Parliament and its leader denounced it as 'a dangerous
interference with academic freedom'. The National Union of
South African Students, representing the English-speaking
students, declared that the proposed 'tribal colleges' would not

be able to search for the truth as their foundation rested on 'a belief in the racial inferiority of the Africans'.

Many professors and lecturers at the universities protested against 'university Apartheid'. Dr. E. G. Malherbe, principal of the Natal University, declared that a stigma was always attached to the degrees attained in what were disparagingly called in the United States 'nigger universities', and there was a danger of the same situation developing in South Africa. Funds were raised both in South Africa and overseas to carry on a campaign against the attempt to deprive the open universities of the right of governing themselves.

The Government was not moved by the storm. In a speech in April 1957 Strijdom said: 'The universities are there to serve the nation and are not apart from and independent of the nation. While we cannot tie the universities down in their research, and in developing the faculties of the students to think independently and to attain knowledge, no Christian nation can, for instance, allow State-supported institutions to undermine the Christian foundations of the State. The nation cannot allow such institutions to spread doctrines that are perilous to the life or future of the White race. For the future of the White race in Southern Africa it is necessary that we develop our country so that it will gradually provide for a bigger White population.'

The Bill was placed before Parliament and then withdrawn and a new one substituted which removed the liability of a university to prosecution if it registered Non-White students in the face of a ban by the Government. Instead the student was liable to prosecution. The Government assumed power to control the entry of Non-White students to all universities. The Bill was fought in all its stages but was eventually passed.

The Strijdom Government took further powers to control the association of Non-Whites and Whites in a wide variety of activities. In 1957 it placed before Parliament the Native Laws Amendment Bill. It was a consolidating measure incorporating three existing Acts. One clause provided that no one conducting schools, hospitals, clubs or similar institutions in a White urban area might grant admittance to Bantu without prior approval of the Minister of Native Affairs and of the urban local authority concerned. The Minister might prohibit such institutions from admitting Bantu if in his opinion the presence of Bantu constituted a nuisance to residents in the vicinity and that the local authority concurred in that opinion. The Minister might also prohibit the admission of Bantu on his sole authority if the institution was conducted in a way prejudicial to the public interest. The Minister might further prohibit the holding of any gathering in a White urban area which was to be attended by Non-Whites if the Minister considered that the gathering would constitute a public nuisance or was undesirable in view of the locality in which it was to be held.

Another clause provided that the Minister of Native Affairs might order, on the recommendation of the local authority concerned, that the attendance by Bantu at any church or other religious service or church function on premises situated within any urban area outside a Bantu residential area should cease from a date to be specified if such attendance was causing a nuisance in the vicinity or if the numbers in which the Bantu attended was considered undesirable. In the event of the Minister's order being disobeyed a Bantu defying such an order would be held responsible before the law. The church concerned must be consulted before any such order was issued.

The Bill also put the sole power for admitting Bantu work-seekers to an urban area into the hands of the Native Labour Bureau. Power was given to prevent the indiscriminate return of seasonal workers to an urban area, or of workers who were born in a particular area but had abandoned residence of that area. A Bantu who was convicted of a crime where the sentence was at least six months' imprisonment or a £50 fine, forfeited the right of residence in a White urban area.

The Bill gave magistrates and Native Commissioners summary power to order the removal of a Bantu from a Bantu township within a White urban area if satisfactory evidence was submitted that such a person had failed to observe the conditions applying to Bantu living in that area.

When the Bill was gazetted the churches interpreted certain clauses to mean that they could be barred from admitting Native worshippers and some of them announced that they would defy such a law. The Government insisted that the Bill did not prevent anyone from worshipping and only sought to ensure that the worship of Europeans in urban areas was not disturbed by Natives coming into the district to enter White churches.

However, a new 'church clause' was drafted under which the onus was not on the churches to obtain permission for Natives to attend services. Under it the Minister had power to bar Natives if a local authority complained that their entry into a White area to attend a church created a nuisance. The Action Committee of the Christian Council of South Africa denounced the new clause as more objectionable than the original one in that 'it penalized the African worshipper rather than the church as a whole'.

The 'church clause' gave rise to long and heated debates in the House of Assembly, but it was carried by 65 votes to 41. It attracted a good deal of attention in Great Britain and cartoons condemning it appeared in *Punch* and other journals. The Nationalists accused the Opposition of working up an unjustified agitation against the measure, and of damaging the reputation of South Africa abroad.

The national committee of the Liberal Party in South Africa passed a resolution stating that in its view 'inter-racial association is a cardinal principle of a democratic multi-racial society' and that therefore it was 'in complete opposition to the Bill'. It also noted 'with the gravest concern' indications that the Government might ban the African National Congress. It considered that such an action 'will drive many of the African people into a position where revolution will appear to them to be the only way of achieving social and political change.'

The United Party criticized the Government's policy on the ground that it was damaging South Africa's good name abroad, was creating a frustrated Black proletariat in the urban areas, was arousing a spirit of African nationalism that would become a danger to the White race and was wilfully destroying every 'bridge' between White and Black.

In defending the measure, Verwoerd, the Minister of Native Affairs, said that it was of the utmost importance to ensure that social integration was not allowed to develop. The possibility of the development of social integration by a general admixture in clubs and institutions and welfare associations was a danger to South Africa. The third reading of the Bill was carried by 79 votes to 48.

Verwoerd told the House of Assembly plainly what he held should be the only relationship between Whites and Natives. 'I accept,' he said, 'that I must have contact with the Native in connection with the office I hold. But it is that of the guardian with the person whom he must uplift. And it will be so throughout the whole of society. When Whites work with Non-Whites in the sphere of social welfare the aim must not be to form common welfare bodies for White and Black but to build up a Bantu welfare service. In the transition period in which the European must give guidance as guardian he must naturally give instruction to the Native who is still inexperienced. But the contact must be on the basis of Apartheid. You do not need to maintain contact by means of mixed meetings . . . What clearly ought not to take stronger root in South Africa, because it clashed directly with the Apartheid policy, is the establishment of multi-racial organizations of mixed bodies.'

Critics of the Government argued that the strict enforcement of the principle would kill, or at least change the character of, a number of associations such as the Joint Councils of Europeans and Natives, the Institute of Race Relations, the Red Cross, the St. John Ambulance and so on. In the early days of Union the professions had received a certain amount of self-government. Doctors, dentists and chemists had professional associations with the power to discipline their members. These societies had no colour bar.

The Nursing Act of 1944 had established a Nursing Council free from a colour bar. In 1957 the parent body, the South African Nursing Association, and the Nursing Council put before a Select Committee of Parliament a scheme introducing colour discrimination in the nursing profession. A Bill was accordingly drafted which made the Nursing Council an all-White body supported by advisory boards of Coloureds, Indians and Natives. The Nursing Council was to keep separate registers for nurses and mid-wives of different races and might prescribe different uniforms and badges and be able to draw up different qualifications or conditions for different classes or persons or different branches of the profession. All nurses of all races would continue to belong to the Nursing Association; but the different races would hold separate meetings and the decisions of the White Nursing Council would be the decisions of the Nursing Association which would establish separate branches or groups for Whites, Coloureds and Natives. The Bill provided that anyone who made or allowed a White nurse to work under a Non-White person in any hospital or similar institution or in any training school, except in cases of emergency, would be liable to a fine of £200.

The Non-European groups of the Nursing Association protested strongly against the Bill and called for racial discrimination in nursing to be made an offence. They opposed the Apartheid clauses in the measure and considered that Non-European nurses were competent to participate directly in all the affairs of the nursing profession. They said that the Bill would cause a lowering of the status and education of nurses with the result that the standard of medicine in Non-European hospitals would deteriorate and the acute shortage of nurses would be accentuated. The Government was not to be convinced and the Bill was passed.

While taking steps to decrease the contacts between Whites and Non-Whites in various spheres, the Strijdom Government assumed additional powers enabling it to deal promptly with subversive movements or organized campaigns calling for resistance to the law.

The Public Safety Act of 1953 had given the Government almost unlimited power even in peace time. It provided that the Governor-General could proclaim a state of emergency whenever he was of opinion that any action by a body of persons seriously threatened the safety of the public or the maintenance of order. The Strijdom Government took still more power to enable it to deal with collective movements or individual actions that might create a disturbance of any kind. It placed on the Statute Book in 1955 the Criminal Procedure and Evidence Amendment Act, one clause of which enabled the police to enter any meeting without a warrant if delay caused by obtaining one might defeat the object of the intended entry.

The Minister of Justice (C. R. Swart) who handled the measure said that the additional power was needed because Communists organized 'private social gatherings' entry to which was gained by tickets which were freely granted to anyone who cared to attend but not to the police. In the previous year the police had been prevented from attending this type of gathering because the organisers obtained an urgent interim interdict from a judge which had the effect of ejecting the police on the day in question despite the fact that a named Communist had been announced as one of the speakers. To avoid uncertainty in the future the police were now to be given the right to attend any meeting whether announced as private or not. The Act gave the police the right to break into a meeting after audibly demanding admission and being refused.

Natives can be excluded or removed from certain areas under the terms of several Acts. The majority of banishments have been ordered under the Native Administration Act under which the

Minister may order the removal of any African from one area to another 'if he deems it expedient in the general public interest'. Such persons may be given reasons for their banishment, but they are not entitled to a trial before a court nor can they seek an interdict to delay their removal.

The Departure from the Union Regulation Act made it an offence for anyone to leave the Union without a passport or permit. The Government explained that this power was taken 'to cramp the style' of Communists and others who went abroad (without passports) to Moscow and other communist centres and carried on propaganda hostile to the Union or returned to carry on subversive activities in the Union.

The Natives (Urban Areas) Amendment Act of 1955 laid down that an employer may not house on his premises more than five Natives without permission. Known as the 'Locations in the Sky' Act, the law aimed at limiting the number of Native servants allowed to live on the top of blocks of flats, thus reducing the number of Natives sleeping in a city. The Act also gave local authorities power to banish Natives from their areas without giving detailed reasons for doing so.

In liberal-minded quarters there was a growing feeling against the Strijdom Government's stricter application of the Apartheid laws, and in April 1957 the members of the National Executive Committee of the Institute of Race Relations issued 'a statement to the nation'. They pointed out that throughout the years the Institute, with many welfare, inter-racial and other organizations, had worked 'to secure the orderly and evolutionary advance of our multi-racial society'. The statement proceeded:

'We are convinced that the policies at present being pursued by the Government of South Africa are destroying any advance made towards these goals and are doing untold damage to our common future. We believe that these policies will fail because they are the negation of right principle. We believe they will defeat themselves because they conflict with our economic structure and jeopardize future economic development. They will fail too because they are inducing among Europeans a widespread unease and distrust in the future of South Africa and are giving rise among Non-Europeans to a mounting tide of resentment of authority and of the White man who exercises that authority. No people can be kept in the strait-jacket of control which the legislation of the past nine years, added to an already repressive legislative structure,

has imposed, and which the Bills at present before Parliament—
the Native Laws Amendment Bill and the Separate University
Education Bill—make even more intolerable. These Bills together
with the directive being issued to welfare organizations aim at
undermining all voluntary European association with Africans and
canalizing all contact through public servants alone. Should this
happen, and should the tide of resentment now running continue,
we believe most sincerely that the outcome will be tragic for all in
our country. With means of voluntary communication increasingly
restricted the racial groups may become sealed off into entirely
separate and hostile camps. It is with a heavy sense of responsibility
and a heart-felt concern for the future of the country that we issue
this grave statement. We call on our fellow South Africans, particularly on the Europeans who exercise sole political power, to
take heed before it is too late.'

The Nationalists insisted that all such protests misrepresented
the Government's policy and that the measures taken would not be
applied in a spirit of hostility to the Non-Whites. They blamed the
Opposition and the newspapers supporting it for the prejudice
against South Africa that existed overseas. The Government's
policy they argued was necessary because 'the salvation of the
White race is at stake'.

The Government claimed that among the Non-Whites there
was a considerable body of opinion in favour of the policy of
separation and that the African and Indian Congresses did not
represent all the people in their communities.

In June 1956 the South African Indian Organization (a less
militant body than the South African Indian Congress) sent a
deputation to the Prime Minister and Dr. Donges and put forward
the following requests: (1) That the pressure on Indians resulting
from the Group Areas Act should be eased in order to provide
better economic opportunities and ensure the continuance of
freedom of contact in trade and industry with other racial groups;
(2) that the Government should give unqualified recognition to the
fact that the Indians are an integral part of the permanent South
African population and thus contribute towards a better and
happier relationship between Indians and other racial groups;
(3) that provision should be made for suitable and adequate farm
lands for Indians so that they may use their skill in farming and
thus contribute to the production of much-needed food for the
country; (4) that the Government should provide for the greater

employment of Indians in the public service; (5) that in the provision of housing, civic amenities and the like by local authorities the Indian people should receive a reasonable share.

The deputation issued a statement declaring that the points put forward 'were received with courtesy by the Prime Minister who said that he would give them his consideration'.

The South African Indian Congress however hotly denounced the Indian Organization for its action in sending a deputation to interview the Prime Minister.

In November 1956 there was a change in the leadership of the Opposition in Parliament. Its leader, J. G. N. Strauss, had to take long leave owing to ill-health, and the United Party congress elected as leader forty-three-year-old Sir David de Villiers Graaff, a prominent Cape farmer and business man whose father had sat in Botha's first Union Ministry.

In his first speech after being elected leader Sir David said that the party believed that there was a place for all individuals in the country no matter of what race. 'We believe,' he went on, 'that the Europeans should in the interests of Western civilization retain the leadership, but to maintain this leadership we must get the confidence, goodwill and co-operation of the Non-European population. If we deny them their place they may turn their back on White civilization. Our policy is not equality. That never has been, and never will be, our policy.'

In the large urban centres of the Union the bulk of the Natives live in locations a considerable distance from their place of employment. Often the only transport available is a bus service run by a private company. In 1956 the company serving the Johannesburg and Pretoria areas raised its fares, and the Natives asserted that they could not afford to pay more. They decided to boycott the buses as from January 7, 1957. In the case of Alexandra township outside Johannesburg, where some 140,000 Natives lived, the boycott meant that thousands of Natives had to walk some nine or ten miles into the city in the morning and the same distance back at night, often in pouring rain. The boycott was so complete that the bus company which had run empty vehicles for a time sent them back to the sheds.

The Minister of Transport was overseas when the boycott began and when he returned he said that the Government was not prepared to intervene and that the boycott must be broken. He suggested that employers could help to bring it to an end by not tolerating late arrival and refusing to pay for time not worked.

Meanwhile the boycott had spread and some 45,000 Natives were refusing to use the buses. The Government exerted all the pressure it could to defeat the boycott. It refused to allow train services to be increased on lines serving the locations. Many Europeans were giving their Native employees lifts; and the police began to stop motor cars carrying Natives and demand the production of drivers' licences and to prosecute anyone with an excess of passengers. A ban was placed on the operation of Native taxis outside the municipal area, and the traffic police even arrested about a hundred Natives for crossing an intersection on foot against the robot before six o'clock in the morning when there was no traffic on the road. Police raids were made on Native townships and municipal hostels where men were sleeping illegally in order to save a long walk to their homes. The Minister of Justice subsequently told Parliament that 6,600 Natives had been arrested while another 7,860 were warned and subpoenaed to pay arrear taxes.

After the boycott had lasted for fourteen weeks a scheme was evolved by which private enterprise paid the extra fares and the Natives rode in the buses again.

Commenting on the whole affair the Director of the Institute of Race Relations wrote: 'What is significant to my mind, and I believe to the minds of many observers, has been the self-discipline of the African people concerned, the solidarity of feeling and opinion and the high degree of communication amongst them. To walk between eighteen and twenty miles a day bespeaks a determination and solidarity which is significant. It is also I think indicative of something else—a new factor, a new psychological attitude which first became apparent to me at the Bloemfontein conference convened to discuss the Tomlinson Report. It is something which is not easy to define precisely. One would say it is a new understanding communally reached by the African people that they must think and act for themselves; a determination that an attitude or decision arrived at after reasoned thought and consideration will be maintained; a new common awareness of common interests and a common passive strength; of a common will not founded on extravagant emotion but on reasoned appraisal. This in my experience is a new factor in the racial situation. The African people have again shown that amazing ability to communicate and organize without an organization which has been apparent on other occasions in the past. *It is significant.*'

The Government put through Parliament the Native Transport Services Act as an urgent measure and it was passed through all its stages in one day. It enabled part of the money derived from the Native Services Act of 1952 to be used for subsidizing transport services.

Strijdom decided to apply the principle of Apartheid more strictly in tram and bus services. In many centres buses were run in which space was made available upstairs, or in the back seats, for Non-Whites. The proprietors stated that to run entirely separate services on all routes at all times would necessitate an increase in fares. Now the Government insisted upon complete segregation being introduced as soon as possible.

The African National Congress group called for a one-day 'work-boycott' on June 26, 1957, the fifth anniversary of the launching of the Defiance Campaign, as a protest against the Apartheid policy, the pass laws and low wages—a minimum rate of £1 a day was demanded. Industrial and commercial firms did their best to persuade their employees not to answer the call, and the Government promised ample police protection to all who went to work. The decision to call a one-day strike had not been unanimous and some of the Native trade unions had protested against it. On the Day of Protest only about forty or fifty per cent of the factory and commercial Native employees on the Rand stayed at home, and in other centres the response was poor.

The Congress organizations then called on the public to boycott the products of firms held to be under the control of members of the National Party. Fourteen brands of cigarettes and tobacco were listed as a start. The companies affected went to the High Court and obtained an interdict restraining the African National Congress from distributing leaflets calling for the boycott. The interdict was extended from time to time; but many Natives avoided dealing with what they regarded as Nationalist firms.

The *baasskap* policy was fought by what was known as the Congress Group consisting of the African National Congress, the South African Indian Congress, the South African Coloured People's Organization, the South African Congress of Trade Unions (multi-racial) and the South African Congress of Democrats (White). The Congress of Democrats is opposed to all forms of inequality and discrimination. It demands for all South Africans the rights proclaimed in the Universal Declaration of Human Rights adopted by the United Nations. These groups aim at the establishment of a multi-racial society brought about by peaceful methods. There is however a section of the African National Congress which favours a more militant policy. Those who call for it are known as Africanists. They desire the setting up of a purely African government on the lines of that established in Ghana.

The African National Congress meeting in 1954 received a report from its Executive Committee which stated: 'Because of the Government's crippling attacks on the Congress, the state of unpreparedness of our people in the face of these attacks, and because of the alarming fluctuations in the membership and the failure to carry out some of our important decisions, it has become imperative that we should place before this conference the question of our organizational problems as the most urgent issue for consideration. Your attention is directed to two important matters that emerge from the report; the growing oppression since the Nationalists came into power in 1948, and the position of the African National Congress in such a situation—in other words the re-organization and the functioning of the A.N.C. under the conditions of a fully-fledged police State in which we live.' It was stated that the Congress appointed a number of leaders ready to take over in the event of the present leaders being arrested or deported to other areas, and that it prepared to go underground in the event of the Government declaring it to be an illegal body.

The Government then took steps to secure still more control of the Natives. Proclamation No. 236 of August 16, 1957, provided that the Minister of Native Affairs or any person acting under his authority, may, whenever he deems it expedient, cancel the right of occupation by any African of any land of which the Native Trust is the registered owner and order him and his family to depart. Should the African fail to comply with the order he will upon conviction be liable to a fine up to £100 or imprisonment for twelve months. An order for the summary removal of the man and his family and property may then be issued.

Then on September 13, 1957, Proclamation No. 283 applied the provisions of the Natives Prohibition of Interdicts Act to all orders issued under Proclamation 236. In other words an African ordered to leave Trust land may not appeal against the order until after he has complied with it. According to the Tomlinson Report

Trust-owned land amounts to 14,564,446 morgen out of 16,621,755 morgen occupied by Africans in the Reserves. The Institute of Race Relations declared that these enactments meant in effect that 'Africans require permission to live anywhere at all'.

A Multi-racial Conference sponsored by a number of prominent citizens was held at the University of the Witwatersrand in December, 1957. It was attended by some eight hundred people, White, Coloured and Black (though Whites were in the majority) half of whom were participants and half observers. The object of the gathering was to 'discuss and explore the steps which can bring about friendly and effective co-operation among the different racial groups'.

On the subject of human relations the Conference declared: 'The danger facing South Africa is that of a headlong collision between the forces of White domination and those of counter-domination. . . . Apartheid offers no solution to this threatening impasse. It offers security to nobody. It condemns White South Africa to live out its historical span behind the walls of a fortress, and it condemns Non-White South Africa to an unrelenting struggle to breach those walls.'

Dealing with political rights, the Conference stated that it was convinced that only universal adult suffrage could meet the needs and aspirations of the people. It added: 'It appreciates however that there is disagreement as to the ways of achieving the transition from White supremacy to an non-racial democracy.'

On economic rights the Conference resolved that 'everyone should have the right to earn his living in any legitimate way according to his skill and ability . . . All colour bars in industry must be abolished and all workers should be entitled to a living wage according to civilized standards.' It added that all workers should have the right to combine in trade unions and to be entitled to strike.

The Conference called for compulsory free education for all and rejected educational policies 'which seek to perpetuate White domination, accentuate ethnic differences and resuscitate tribal nationalism.'

A general election was due in 1958 and the different parties prepared to fight it on the colour issue. The National Party promised the continued enforcement of the Apartheid policy as the only way of preserving White supremacy in South Africa. It declared that the policy of the United Party must in the end result in the domination of the Non-Whites. The spirit of the Nationalists was shown by Verwoerd when he addressed the Free State Nationalists on the eve of the polling. He said that the education of the Natives in the Western way of life had led to some of them wanting to become part and parcel of the European community. The Government intended within five or ten years to put an end to that class of Native. 'We will,' he said, 'use an iron hand with regard to mixed gatherings aimed at undermining the Government's Apartheid policy.'

Polling day had been fixed for April 16, and there was a movement among the Bantu in favour of marking the occasion by some action protesting against the fact that they could take no part in the governing of the country. What was called a 'national workers conference' was convened by the African National Conference and it voted for 'mass action' two days before polling day in the form of a stay-at-home strike and demonstrations and processions. There was also a demand for a minimum wage of £1 a day.

As soon as the idea of united action by Non-Whites was mooted Strijdom warned the African National Congress that all possible steps were being taken by the Government to deal with the suggested stay-at-home strike. A committee of heads of departments had been formed and instructed to ensure that if a labour disturbance was created the mass of the peace and order-loving Non-White workers would not be interfered with and essential services would be maintained. He appealed to employers to take drastic action against agitators and strikers 'so that Leftists and Communist agitators will be taught a lesson'.

The Government banned all gatherings of more than ten Bantu for an indefinite period in all the main urban centres of the Union. At the same time the police of the Security Branch raided the offices of several of the Congress organizations and several arrests were made. The African National Congress was also banned from numerous Bantu Reserves in the Transvaal.

A few days before the stay-at-home movement was due to begin, several of the Bantu trade union leaders pronounced against it. In the event, the response to the appeal to stay at home was so small that before the end of the day the African National Congress advised its supporters to return to work owing to the 'punitive measures' taken by the Government and the 'economic pressure and propaganda' of employers.

The threat of a Native strike probably helped the Nationalists

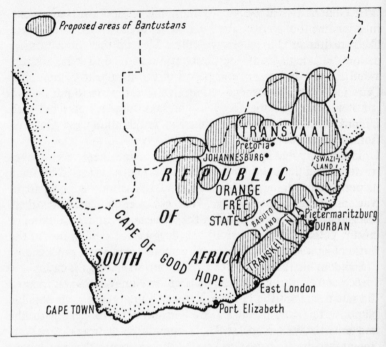

Proposed areas of Bantustans

THE RINGED AREAS SHOW ROUGHLY THE BANTU HOMELANDS PLANNED
IN SOUTH AFRICA UNDER THE SEPARATE DEVELOPMENT SCHEME.

who blamed the United Party for the more aggressive attitude of
the Non-Whites. At the polls the Government won an outstanding
victory. The National Party gained 103 seats against 94 in 1953,
and the United Party strength in the House of Assembly fell from
57 to 53. The Labour Party lost all the five seats it had won in
1953. Never before had a political party in the Union been given
a third five-year term of office in succession. The electorate was
evidently not in a mood to sanction any weakening of the Apartheid
policy.

The Strijdom Government adopted a stiffer attitude towards the
United Nations at whose gatherings there had for several years
been a growing disposition to criticize the colour policy of the
Union. The Union delegates insisted that under Article 2(7) of its
Charter the question was a domestic one in which no other country
had a right to interfere.

Article 14 of the United Nations Charter declared, however:

'The General Assembly may recommend measures for the peaceful adjustment of any situation regardless of origin which it deems likely to impair the general welfare or friendly relations among nations.' Taking advantage of this clause the delegates from India asked for the inclusion on the agenda of an item entitled 'The Question of the Treatment of Indians in South Africa.'

Later, other delegates from Non-White countries criticized the Union's colour policy and a three-member United Nations Commission was appointed to study the racial situation in the Union. Ultimately after several protests against interference with its domestic affairs the Union withdrew its delegates and recalled its permanent representative from the headquarters of the United Nations. The Nationalists held that some of the Non-European delegates to the United Nations raised the question of the Union's colour policy for political and propaganda purposes and that further argumentation with them would be useless.

Strijdom visited South-West Africa at the end of 1955 and in a speech at Windhoek said that he was convinced that the territory did not desire to become a mandated territory under the United Nations. The Union and South-West Africa had become a unity and must in future be regarded as one country and one nation. Soon after his visit the administration of Bantu affairs in South-West Africa was taken over by the Union's Bantu Affairs Department. This step had repercussions in the General Assembly of the United Nations. Some of the African delegates declared that the Union Government was not carrying out its mandate as far as the Natives were concerned. They said that South-West Africa ought to be placed under the trusteeship of the United Nations, and asked that negotiations should be begun for arranging the transfer. The Union Government refused to allow delegates from the United Nations to visit South-West Africa.

Strijdom attended the new session of the Union Parliament after the general election, and on July 8 spoke on a vote of no-confidence moved by the Opposition. On July 11 it was announced that he had had a recurrence of his heart complaint and had been ordered a complete rest.

A few days later he was admitted to hospital, and he died there on August 24, 1958.

CHAPTER X

Verwoerd Creates Bantustans

The death of Hans Strijdom made it necessary for the National Party to elect a new leader who would be invited to form a Ministry.

The choice was a matter of special importance because it was clear that a definite and sustained policy on the relations of Black and White must be applied at once. The wave of African nationalism was lapping the walls of the Union, and the danger could no longer be ignored. Either the foundations of a multi-racial society must be laid, or colour separation must be placed on a permanent basis by giving the Blacks their own areas in which they could develop to the full extent of their capacity.

For such an Hour the majority in the National Party saw in Dr. H. F. Verwoerd the Necessary Man. As Minister of Native Affairs for eight years he had built up a reputation as a leader who could devise a bold logical policy and enforce it ruthlessly in the face of sustained opposition. And so the Nationalists entrusted their future to a man who lacked the qualification of long party service which had counted for so much in calmer days, and who was not even a South African by birth.

Indeed Verwoerd's succession to the Nationalist throne was almost a miracle. In 1948 he was a defeated candidate for Parliament. In 1958 he was Prime Minister. He had only been an elected member of Parliament for four months—before that he had been a nominated Senator.

Hendrick Frensch Verwoerd was born near Amsterdam in Holland on September 8, 1901. He was brought to the Union with his family when he was two years old. He had a brilliant scholastic career and studied at universities in Europe and the United States before becoming the head of the Department of Sociology at the University of Stellenbosch. Later he was editor of a Nationalist newspaper in Johannesburg until he was given a seat in the Senate where he led for the Malan Government and received the portfolio of Native Affairs.

One of his first acts as Prime Minister was to make a small but significant change in the naming of departments. Several of the English-language papers had adopted the practice of referring to the Natives as 'Africans'. The Nationalists protested against the Bantu being called Africans, and in Parliament Verwoerd refused to answer any questions about 'Africans', saying that he did not know of any such race. So immediately he became Prime Minister he would not even have a Minister and Department of Native Affairs. He had a Minister of Bantu Administration and Development and a Minister of Bantu Education, both with Deputy Ministers. In Government circles the word Africans is now never used. The Blacks are called Bantu and sometimes Natives, but never Africans.

Verwoerd made his colour policy plain. In reply to criticism in Parliament he said: 'Dr. Malan said it, and Mr. Strijdom said it, and I have said it repeatedly and I want to say it again: The policy of Apartheid moves consistently in the direction of more and more separate development with the ideal of total separation in all spheres. Everyone realizes that it is not practicable at the present moment, that it cannot be attained in a few years, but everyone realizes at the same time that if you have a clear and definite ideal in view—whether you have one moving towards separate development even territorially—it can be advanced even in these times.'

When Verwoerd became Prime Minister Black nationalism was sweeping across the African continent. Ghana had become an independent State. The French colonies had been made independent communities with the right to secede from the French Union if they chose. The Belgians were promising the Congo self-government. Nigeria was about to be granted home rule. In every Native area there were heard cries for 'Freedom'.

Verwoerd was alive to the importance of the awakening of the African giant. 'We must,' he said, 'draw a line in Africa between these territories to be controlled by the White man and those to be controlled by the Black man. It is unlikely that White control will remain in Tanganyika, Kenya, the Congo or the Portuguese territories. The line of White control may not even cover the Central African Federation judging by the speeches of some of its leaders. South Africa does not plan to solve its colour problem by oppression. The solution must of necessity also offer advantages to the Bantu and the Coloured.' Among the advantages he offered were five universities for the Bantu, the Coloureds and the Asiatics.

His master plan for the separation of Whites and Blacks was revealed in the terms of the Promotion of Bantu Self-Government Bill which he forced through Parliament in 1959 by 102 votes to 58.

The Government explained that its philosophy in these matters rested on three corner stones:

(a) God had given a divine task and calling to every nation.
(b) Every nation had an inherent right of self-preservation.
(c) The personal and national ideals of every individual and of every population group could best be developed within its own political community. Only then would other groups feel that they were not endangered.

The Preamble of the Bill made it clear that the Government did not consider the Bantu a homogeneous people but a number of separate national units on the basis of language and culture. It was desirable for the welfare and progress of the Bantu that this should be recognized. The Bill therefore contemplated the creation of eight main national homelands in which the Bantu would be able to develop to their full capacity as independent communities. By the establishment of Bantu territorial authorities over their land the Bantu would be stimulated to govern themselves. The powers of the territorial authorities to be set up included the right to tax their own people, to establish markets and pounds, control public works and allocate licences and trading rights.

The Bantu in the White areas, however, would not be permanent residents even if they were born there and worked there all their life. They would remain citizens of the Bantu areas, and would be 'interchangeable' with the dwellers in the Bantu homelands, to which it was believed they would eventually retire. In each of these Bantu areas the Government would be represented by a Commissioner-General whose duty it would be to explain Government policy and promote the development of their areas. Administration in the Bantu homelands would be based on the tribal system, and the Government retained the right to approve of all appointments of chiefs and headmen and to veto any action with which it disagreed. It would also control the schools and colleges or universities to be established. Gradually all European judicial officers and European agricultural officers, teachers and administrative officers would be replaced by qualified and competent Bantu.

The Opposition in Parliament, and the public, promptly called these Bantu national units 'Bantustans'.

Verwoerd's plan was explained in a White Paper which stated that 'the first irrevocable steps' in the establishment of Bantu territorial units had been taken and that the Government was 'moving to a further stage of this process'.

The White Paper asserted that the realization of the political autonomy envisaged for the Bantu units demanded that all factors which retarded such development should be removed systematically. When the matter was examined from that angle it appeared that the greatest impediment was the representation of the Bantu in the highest institutions of European government, an impediment which moreover was of a twofold nature. 'On the one hand,' declared the White Paper, 'it is the source of European fears of being swamped by the Bantu in the political sphere, and on the other hand it fails to stimulate the development of Bantu institutions because it fosters expectations of greater participation in political institutions and promotes the desertion of trained human material from service within its own community.'

It was then argued that representation in the guardian's Parliament played no part in the attainment of self-government in the British Commonwealth and was 'in effect a sign-post to the alternative direction which has been rejected as utterly impracticable'. The White Paper claimed that under the Bantu authorities system the Bantu already played an increasingly important part in all facets of community development. It proceeded: 'For the first time in their history the Bantu realize that the European is prepared to grant them full freedom of progress within their own sphere of life and that it is not the European's intention to retard the assignment of powers to them on the ground that the time is not ripe but that it is the firm intention to give them all the training required for this purpose.'

The Nationalists insisted that the foundations of these Bantu national homes had already been laid. Towns or villages were being marked out. The inhabitants of the units were being taught better methods of cultivating the soil and were being instructed in the growing of crops, such as sisal, which would become the basis of small industries. The Bantu Investment Corporation with a capital of £500,000 would be formed to assist the Bantu in in starting their own commercial enterprises.

During the debates in Parliament Verwoerd outlined his plan in more detail. The Government's scheme, he said, would lead to a permanent White South Africa with separate Bantu national units which could develop into independent Bantu States but which the Government believed could be bound to the White State through wise statesmanship, help and co-operation. If and when the Bantu areas developed into autonomous units they would be politically independent, though there would be economic inter-dependence. He was convinced that the development of the Bantu national homes would create so much friendship that there would be no danger of animosity towards White South Africa. On the contrary he foresaw a commonwealth of common interests as was the case with the European Common Market.

The Prime Minister went on to argue that unless the Government's plan was accepted the only other choice was a common multi-racial country where the Whites would be outnumbered by the Blacks by three or four to one. If this were the only other choice he had no hesitation in choosing a smaller White State rather than a big State which would eventually become Non-White. In the smaller State the White man would at least be able to control his own territory and work out his own destiny. He agreed that there might be some dangers for the future, but it was his deep conviction that these proposed States and their Bantu peoples would be so grateful for what had been done for them, and that there would be so many mutual interests and so much co-operation, that they, with the Union, would become a sub-continent bound together by community of interests and goodwill.

'It must be realized,' he continued, 'once and for all that the development in the Bantu areas will begin with what they themselves know and with what is their own, and it will grow and be adapted to the demands of modern civilization by the Bantu themselves with whatever aid the Whites can give.'

He asserted that it was incorrect to say that no rights would be given to the Bantu working and living in the White areas. They would have rights in the control of their own ethnic units in the Bantu areas, and machinery would be created in place of advisory boards which would give the Bantu control over their local affairs —not in the same degree as the Coloured people would be given municipal rights in their areas, but they would be given a voice in their local affairs. The Bantu in the urban centres would not be considered permanent residents of the White areas. They would be replaceable, and would be able to return to the Bantu areas where the knowledge they had acquired could be used to the benefit of their own people. They too would enjoy certain rights. Their political rights would be connected with their homelands, while in their residential areas around the White urban areas they would be granted limited control of their own affairs under the guardianship of White municipalities.

Verwoerd's plan for the establishment of Bantu national homes as a solution of the colour problem was received with enthusiasm by the Nationalists. Their newspapers acclaimed it as giving a 'new look' to Apartheid which would make it acceptable to the world.

For years the Nationalists had heard themselves denounced by oversea publicists and delegates to the United Nations for oppressing the Non-Whites and striving to make permanent an unjust colour discrimination such as existed nowhere else on the globe. Criticism from so many quarters worried the supporters of the Government, and they looked for an answer that would once and for all remove the stigma which they felt was being unjustly placed upon South Africa. They believed that the 'new look' given to their traditional policy of colour separation provided such an answer.

Verwoerd insisted that so far from employing the methods of a bygone and discredited age the Union Government was actually leading the world in conferring freedom and full opportunities for development upon backward peoples. The British Government, he asserted, was being lauded for training its colonial Natives for home rule. But it was now clear that the Union's policy did precisely the same thing—only it did it better. In Basutoland, for instance, the British plan for ultimate home rule permitted Whites to remain in the country who might exploit the Natives. But under his scheme Basutoland would be reserved exclusively for the Basutos and no Whites would be allowed to live in it, much less conduct businesses that might otherwise be carried on by the Natives. Thus, were Basutoland transferred to the Union, its people would enjoy a greater measure of self-government than they would have were they to remain under British rule.

Mr. de Wet Nel, the Minister for Bantu Administration, told

Parliament that there would be the closest co-operation between the Bantu States and the Union, but matters such as defence and foreign affairs would be in the hands of the South African Government, though there would be discussions at the highest level—'similar to the present-day Commonwealth talks'.

Later Verwoerd said that the Bantu units might become entirely independent States, and de Wet Nel admitted that that might be so. Other Nationalists however declared that it would take two thousand years before the Bantu would be fitted to run independent States.

The Transkei with about a million-and-a-half Natives was proclaimed the first Bantu national home. It includes several White towns and numerous White store-keepers. According to the Government these 'White spots' will ultimately have to go; though the White traders were given an assurance that they could remain as long as they liked, but when they gave up business Black traders would take their place.

The United Party asserted that the Bantustans would divide and ruin the country. Industrialists protested against the idea of moving factories to the borders of the Reserves so the Natives would work in them and live in their own area.

The Government however insisted that the Apartheid policy would be pursued because it was the only one by which the supremacy of the Whites in their own areas could be guaranteed. It applied a more constructive policy than its predecessors had done. Natives were trained as builders and employed in erecting thousands of houses in new townships in the industrial areas. Two universities were built for Africans, one at Turfloop in the Northern Transvaal, and the other at Ngoye in Zululand. The Government appointed the professors and lecturers, and the students were strictly controlled and were not allowed to hold meetings, or make statements to the Press, or bring visitors to the hostels without permission.

The Students Representative Council of the Witwatersrand University denounced the regulations as a flagrant violation of student freedoms. They said that the rules confirmed their worst fears, and that the Government was apparently 'unable to distinguish between the type of control required for Universities and reformatories'.

Several Chambers of Commerce and Industry expressed the fear that the creation of Bantustans and the moving of industries to their borders would check the expansion of industry in the Union and make investors shy of putting money into Union concerns.

The opposition to the Government's policy was broadened by the formation of the Progressive Party which pledged itself to the building up of a multi-racial society in which there would be no discrimination on the ground of colour alone. The new organization was launched by members of the United Party who felt that its programme did not differ sufficiently from that of the Nationalists on the colour issue.

Verwoerd had only been Prime Minister for a few months when he had to deal with serious disturbances in Native areas in different parts of the country.

On February 26, 1959, there was rioting in the Lady Selborne location at Pretoria over the issue of passes to Native women. The police charged with batons and opened fire and more than ninety Bantu were injured.

On June 19 at Cato Manor, outside Durban, there was trouble over the destruction of illicit stills on which many Native women relied for a living. The police opened fire and four Natives were killed and thirteen wounded.

On August 15 at Maritzburg, in Natal, Native women protested against restrictions on the earning power of their husbands. There was rioting, and the police intervened and two Natives were killed and one injured.

On November 11 at Paarl, in the Cape, a crowd of Natives protested against the banishment of their trade union leaders. Violence began and the police fired and twelve Natives were wounded.

On December 11 at Windhoek, in South-West Africa, the Herero tribesmen rioted on being moved to a new township. The police fired and twelve were killed and thirty-eight injured.

On March 21, 1960, a large crowd of Natives moved towards the police station at Sharpeville location outside Vereeniging, an industrial town near the Rand. The police thought they were going to rush the station and without orders opened fire, and sixty-nine Natives were killed and 186 wounded.

On March 21 violence broke out at night in the Langa location outside Cape Town, and in a police charge two Natives were killed and forty-nine injured.

On March 28 there were 'Day of Mourning' riots in the Native townships outside Johannesburg and two policemen were killed.

On March 29 houses and churches were set alight at a Native village outside Worcester, in the Cape.

On March 30, at two o'clock in the morning, the police arrested one hundred Black and White people in different parts of the country. The Government proclaimed a State of Emergency in eighty magisterial districts with a population of six millions and called up several Active Citizen Force regiments to stand by. Thousands of heavily armed troops were sent to seal off Langa location at Cape Town from which thirty thousand Non-Whites had marched into the city and caused much alarm, though they were persuaded to go back before trouble started.

On April 1 three Natives were killed when the police opened fire to halt a mob marching into Durban.

The Sharpeville shooting was strongly condemned in Britain, where a fund was opened for the wounded and the relatives of the killed.

The State of Emergency which the Government decreed on March 30 was not lifted until August 31. Under the emergency regulations penalties as high as a fine of £500 or five years' imprisonment, or both, could be imposed. It was estimated that about twenty-three thousand people of all races were arrested during the State of Emergency, though some twenty-one thousand were said to be 'vagrants' arrested under the pass and urban areas laws in a drive to clear the Native townships of idlers and potential criminals.

Verwoerd told Parliament that the widespread rioting had resulted from attempts to organize a 'massive revolt'. He appointed two judges to enquire into the Sharpeville and Langa riots. Broadly, their reports condemned the Native leaders for irresponsibility. The judicial report on the Sharpeville riot found that the police firing had not been justified by the attitude of the crowd.

At the next session of Parliament the Government put through a measure to protect itself against claims for damages arising out of the riots. Non-Whites had entered claims against the Government aggregating tens of thousands of pounds. The Government however set up a committee with power to assess compensation for the relatives of the killed and also for the wounded.

During the Emergency some fifty Natives and Coloureds and a

few Whites escaped to neighbouring territories and gradually made their way to Great Britain. They later formed a central organization pledged to influence public opinion abroad against the Union's colour policy. They appealed to African and Asian countries to work for the ejection of the Union from the United Nations and the British Commonwealth.

The Verwoerd Government declared that innocent Bantu had in the disturbances been subjected to intimidation and a reign of terror. So in the 1960 session of Parliament it put through the Unlawful Organizations Act which empowered the Governor-General (in practice the Government) to declare by proclamation the African National Congress and the Pan-African Congress, or any organization carrying on their functions, an illegal organization. Under the Act sentences for intimidation were increased from a fine of £50 or six months' imprisonment to a maximum sentence of a fine of £500, or five years' imprisonment, or ten lashes, or a combination of these penalties. The Government said that the activities of the two named organizations 'bordered on revolution'. As soon as the Act became law the Government declared them to be illegal bodies.

For several months, however, Verwoerd could not take an active part in affairs. On April 3, 1960, he opened the Union Exposition in Johannesburg. He had just finished his speech when David Pratt, a well-to-do local man, stepped up to him and shot him twice in the head with a revolver. Fortunately the weapon was of small calibre, and Verwoerd made a remarkable recovery, regaining his former good health save for deafness in his right ear. Many Afrikaners regarded his escape as evidence that a Higher Hand had preserved his life in order that he should continue his task of ensuring the survival of the Afrikaner people. His assailant was found to be mentally unbalanced and was sent to an institution.

From January 1, 1960, the income tax law was extended to the Natives in order to provide additional funds for their schools. The change was criticized in Parliament on the ground that the Bantu were treated more harshly than the Whites. They had to begin paying on an income of £180 per annum, whereas unmarried White people earning less than £250 a year, and married ones earning less than £300, paid no income tax at all. Inquiries into the economic position of the Natives showed that £21 per month represented the basic unavoidable expenditure on necessities in urban areas, and that one million African men working in secondary and tertiary industries earned an average of £6 per month too little to maintain minimum standards of living. The result was widespread malnutrition among the Bantu living in the towns. Moreover, while better housing was provided in the new Bantu townships the rents were higher and the cost of transport heavier. Many private firms admitted that Native wages were too low and raised them substantially.

Overseas criticism of the racial policy in South Africa grew both in volume and intensity. Among the bodies condemning it was the International Commission of Jurists, a non-political organization which drew its support from some thirty-seven thousand judges, lawyers and teachers of law in eighty countries. It conducted a lengthy investigation into the situation in the Union and sent its report to the United Nations and to Governments throughout the world.

Its report was published in 1960. It said that the Union Government had established a network of legislation 'which denies to a vast majority of the population those opportunities without which the legitimate aspirations and dignity of a human being cannot be realized'. It declared that such a discriminatory policy 'is not only contrary to generally accepted concepts of justice and principles of human rights but also creates a potentially explosive situation which might soon lead to even more widespread internal violence than has already been experienced.'

The Verwoerd Government dismissed all such attacks on the ground that those who made them did not understand the peculiar situation which existed in South Africa. It said that though Bantu living in the White areas in the Union had to comply with certain regulations as a condition of working there, they had complete freedom in their own areas. It thought that the use of the word Apartheid had been unfortunate and gave a wrong impression abroad. Thereafter it was never employed in official statements, and the term 'separate development' was substituted as the description of the country's policy. In 1961 the South African Broadcasting Corporation decided that 'self-government' must always be used on the air instead of Apartheid.

A number of Afrikaner 'intellectuals', especially in the universities, began to criticize the Apartheid policy, and even in the Dutch churches there were signs that a more liberal school of thought was emerging. In December 1960 a conference of eight South African Protestant churches—including the three Dutch

Churches—sponsored by the World Council of Churches, was held in Johannesburg. It was attended by eighty South African churchmen and a six-man delegation from the World Council. The statement issued after the conference showed that at least eighty per cent of the delegates had agreed to the following points:

(1) There are no scriptural grounds for the prohibition of mixed marriages.

(2) Migrant labour has 'disintegrating effects' on Bantu life.

(3) The wages received by the vast majority of the Non-White people oblige them to exist well below the generally accepted minimum standard for healthy living.

(4) The present system of job reservation must give way to a more equitable system of labour which safeguards the interests of all concerned.

(5) The right to own land wherever he is domiciled, and to participate in the government of the country, is part of the dignity of the adult man, and for this reason a policy which permanently denies to Non-White people the right of collaboration in the government of the country of which they are citizens cannot be justified.

The majority of the ministers and members of the three Dutch Reformed Churches strongly condemned these propositions, and many church gatherings were held at which they were rejected and the delegates from the Dutch Churches who had agreed to them were sharply rebuked.

The report on the 1960 Census showed that the Bantu population had increased faster than had been expected. The total population of the Union was found to be 15,841,128. The number of Whites was 3,067,628, an increase of sixteen per cent over 1951. The Bantu numbered 10,807,809, an increase of 2,247,726, or twenty-six per cent. The Coloureds numbered 1,488,267, an increase of thirty-five per cent. The Asiatics were put at 477,414.

The large increase in the Bantu figures was said to be due to under-enumeration at the 1951 census.

Thus the total Non-White population in 1960 was 12,773,440, or more than four to one over the Whites. Moreover, in the urban areas, despite the influx control during eight years of Apartheid, the Non-White population was seen to be increasing twice as fast as the White population. Pretoria, the administrative capital, which had boasted that it was the only city in the Union with more

Whites than Blacks, was now shown to have a Black majority of 305.

The Opposition quoted the census figures to prove that the Apartheid policy was a failure. The Government replied by speeding up its development measures in the Bantu areas. More money was advanced for the starting of small industries, although the Government still insisted that only Bantu could be allowed to operate them and turned down the suggestion that Whites should be allowed to invest money in industrial development in the Reserves. Five Commissioners-General were appointed for the Bantustans; and the Minister for Bantu Development said that fifty towns would be created in the Reserves, in which, he predicted, there would in time be cities as large as Cape Town or Durban.

Serious unrest however broke out in Pondoland, a district in the Transkei. The tribesmen resented some of the measures enforced by the Bantu authorities and huts were burned down and men murdered, while White traders in some of the Transkei towns were boycotted. A State of Emergency was proclaimed in parts of Pondoland and battalions of the Mobile Watch, a part of the army specially trained to deal with riots, with armoured vehicles and aeroplanes, were moved in. There were clashes with the troops and the police, and a number of Natives were shot. The Government denied that the disturbances were due to resentment at the policy of the Bantu authorities and insisted that it was the work of 'inciters' from outside the area. There were rumours that arms were being landed on the coast, and warships were sent to watch potential landing places. During the operations 4,769 Natives and two Whites were arrested on various charges. Most of them were sent to detention camps.

At Cato Manor, in Natal, a police party searching for illicit liquor was attacked by hundreds of Natives and nine policemen were killed. Apart from this outbreak, the Native townships were quiet. Many of the Congress leaders had been imprisoned, or sent to detention camps, or prohibited from taking part in public gatherings, and for months there was no active opposition to the Government's policy. In Cape Town several groups of Coloured people entered White restaurants and sat down and asked to be served. The police arrested some of them, but when the cases came into court the charges were withdrawn.

Some of the Nationalists in the Cape felt that it would be wise to draw the million-and-a-half Coloured people to the side of the Whites and suggested that the Coloureds should be given the right to elect men of their own race to represent them in the Union Parliament. Verwoerd bluntly refused to consider any such concession; but he outlined plans for developing the Coloured areas and giving the people in them a measure of local self-government. 'In these Coloured urban residential areas,' he said, 'all occupations and activities of the Coloureds must be protected, and they must be given preference regarding trade and other licences. In these centres the Coloureds will have their own educational facilities, sports centres and recreation centres. They will also have their own public services like post offices, police stations, etc.'

Verwoerd declared that development plans on the same lines could also be considered for the Indians 'should they show signs of co-operation on that basis'.

The Coloured people declared that despite many promises nothing had been done to 'lessen the agony of being thrown out of our homes, or seeing our matriculated children pedalling messenger cycles or making tea in city offices while the country cries out for more skill and more educated people'. They launched a new Coloured National Convention movement to co-operate with the Africans and the Indians in fighting the Apartheid policy.

By hard experience the Government found that the Group Areas Act was complicated and ineffective and led to many appeals to the courts. The original 1950 Act was amended six times before a consolidating Act was passed in 1957. In the 1961 session of Parliament twenty-nine of the forty-eight clauses of the consolidated Act were further amended. In many towns the White traders asked for the enforcement of the Act in order to get their Indian rivals moved to Indian townships far out on the veld where their businesses could not be carried on upon a profitable basis. The new Act eased the position of the Indians by laying down that an Indian ordered to live in a distant township could still continue to carry on his business in a White area.

The Government's racial policy continued to be strongly criticized abroad. Harold Macmillan, the British Prime Minister, paid a short visit to the Union early in 1960 and addressed a joint sitting of both Houses of Parliament. He made his famous speech in which he spoke of the 'wind of change' blowing down Africa and said that Great Britain could not support the colour policy of the Union. His pronouncement came as a shock to the Nationalists, and their newspapers accused Britain of 'selling South Africa down the river' and as regarding the Whites in Africa as 'expendable' in order to obtain the trade of the new African States.

Then the United Nations General Assembly instructed its General Secretary, Dag Hammerskold, to visit the Union and try to persuade its Government to modify its policy. He arrived in January 1961 and made a short tour of the country and had long talks with Verwoerd. Their conversations were officially described as 'fruitful', and it was suggested that Hammerskold should pay another visit to the Union; but the Government did not change its colour policy in the slightest degree.

The Union was boycotted by legislative measures in India, Jamaica, Antigua, Barbadoes, the Sudan, Ghana, Malaya, Netherlands New Guinea (Surinam) and Ethiopia. The Union Government announced that it would in no circumstances negotiate with any foreign Government or party responsible for boycott movements against the Union in an attempt to persuade them to abandon such movements.

In a number of other countries, liberal bodies and South Africans in exile asked the public not to buy South African products and so bring pressure upon the Union to modify its colour laws. The Union Government published figures to show that all these boycott efforts had had practically no effect upon the country's exports. Some industries however admitted that their sales overseas had decreased.

While maintaining a running fight against the critics of his racial policy abroad, Verwoerd decided to convert the Union into a republic. A referendum on the issue was taken on October 5, 1960. Only Whites were to vote; and much to the surprise of many people those in South-West Africa were allowed to take part in the poll. The returns showed 850,458 votes for a republic, and 775,878 against—a majority of 74,580 for a republic.

A Bill was then put through Parliament making May 31, 1961, the day on which the republic was to come into being. Very little change was made in the constitution, but a President, elected for seven years, was to take the place of the Queen. The Union flag was to be retained, although many of the Nationalists would have preferred one that did not show the Union Jack even in miniature.

Verwoerd wanted the republic to remain within the British

Commonwealth. When the Prime Ministers' Conference met in London in March 1961 he attended it, and asked that the Republic of South Africa, to be established on May 31, should retain its place as a member. The British Government had no objection, and at first it was thought that permission would be readily granted. During the referendum the Government spokesmen had strongly stressed the point that the republic would be 'within the Commonwealth'. Even while the Union's colour policy was being denounced in the Prime Ministers' Conference the South African Broadcasting Corporation sent out a message saying that the Union was 'in' on certain conditions.

But as soon as the subject of South Africa's membership was introduced, nearly all the Prime Ministers bitterly attacked the Union's Apartheid measures. The British Prime Minister made a sustained attempt to find a formula that would enable a republican South Africa to remain in the Commonwealth and yet record the abhorrence of Apartheid felt by the other members. The discussion lasted for fifteen hours spread over two days, and then, on the evening of March 15, Verwoerd, who had taken the stand all along that his membership of the Commonwealth must be unconditional, suddenly rose and withdrew his application that South Africa should retain its membership of the Commonwealth after it became a republic on May 31, 1961.

In a brief speech he said: 'No self-respecting member of any voluntary organization could, in view of what is being suggested, and the degree of interference shown in what are South Africa's domestic affairs, be expected to wish to retain membership in what is now becoming a pressure group.' He went on to say that it was with great regret that he was obliged to take that step. He felt the character of the Commonwealth had changed completely during the last year. 'The opposition to South Africa's membership of the Commonwealth,' he added, 'is based on alleged discrimination against, and oppression of, the Non-White peoples of South Africa. I do not intend to repeat my strong denial of those allegations. I do, however, wish to state that it is ironical that those allegations have come from Prime Ministers in whose own countries oppression and discrimination are openly practised, and where the basic principles of democratic government are flouted.'

Verwoerd named as those countries Ghana, India, Malaya and Ceylon, though he added that certain other Commonwealth countries were not free from such practices, which were sanctioned by legal enactments. His last words to the other Prime Ministers were: 'In conclusion I wish to state that the proceedings of the final meeting, which have obliged me to take this regrettable step, in my opinion mark the beginning of the disintegration of the Commonwealth'.

The conference had been held behind closed doors, but it was known that Verwoerd had tried hard, with patience and good temper, to devise a formula that would satisfy the members. Indeed all the Press watchers outside predicted that a compromise would be reached enabling South Africa to retain its membership of the 'club'. In the Union it was generally believed that he would succeed, and the news that he had failed had a stunning effect. The value of the shares listed on the Johannesburg Stock Exchange fell heavily.

Among the public the first reaction ran upon politico-party lines. Although the Nationalists had expected that South Africa would remain in the Commonwealth, they gave unanimous support to their leader, and the Dutch Reformed Churches congratulated him on the stand he had taken and promised him full backing in any measures he might deem necessary to safeguard the country.

The Opposition parties deplored the Prime Minister's action and expressed the hope that at a later date South Africa would be able to return to the Commonwealth.

The leaders of the Bantu rejoiced at the exclusion of the Union from the Commonwealth, which they said showed that world opinion was against Apartheid. They felt, too, that with South Africa outside the Commonwealth there would be increased pressure overseas to compel its Government to change its racial policy. Though their organizations had been declared illegal bodies, plans were made for making mass protests against Apartheid and the change to a republican constitution.

Among the English section, however, there were many who sided with Verwoerd. They were alarmed at the massacres in the Congo, the outbreaks of violence in the Rhodesias, and the unrest among the Bantu in the Union, and felt that the Verwoerd Government could be relied upon to 'keep the Native in his place'. A good many people who had hitherto been supporters of the United Party declared that on that ground they could not oppose the Government.

There were debates in the British Parliament on the withdrawal of South Africa, and members of the Government expressed their dislike of Apartheid in strong terms. The Prime Minister (Harold Macmillan) said that the Union's policy seemed to be altogether remote from, and indeed abhorrent to, the ideals for which mankind was struggling in this century. 'It was not,' he added, 'because all of us were without sin that we felt so strongly, but because this theory of Apartheid transposes what we regard as a wrong into a right.'

The Secretary for Commonwealth Relations (Duncan Sandys) said that everywhere governments were trying progressively to eliminate racial discrimination, yet in South Africa discrimination and segregation had been elevated into an objective policy, something to be proud of, an inspiring ideal. He pointed out that South Africa still firmly refused to receive diplomatic representatives from the Non-White States in the Commonwealth. This had made 'a mockery of consultation'. 'In any case,' he added, 'we cannot accept, because of the colour of their skin, that certain members of the Commonwealth are to be treated as lepers.' South Africa had progressively isolated herself, with the result that she had no circle of friends whom she could bring into the common pool.

In the House of Lords, on the other hand, several peers expressed sympathy with South Africa. Lord Fraser of Lonsdale, said that Apartheid did not differ in essence from partition—a policy which had commended itself in India, Ireland and Israel. Apartheid had a positive side, and it was not inconceivable that when history came to be written in another thirty or fifty years those who judged the matter might then be glad there was 'a strong nation preserving law and order at the Southern end of the African continent'.

The British Government made it clear that it despaired of getting Verwoerd to modify his policy in the slightest degree. Sir de Villiers Graaf therefore proclaimed a definite colour programme which the Opposition would place before the country. He appealed to the Whites to unite on five points:

(1) The Coloureds should be accepted as part of the Western community.
(2) The claims of the Indian population should be determined by negotiation with them.
(3) A distinction should be drawn between tribal Natives and Natives who had permanently pulled up their roots in the Reserves.
(4) The Reserves should be developed vigorously with an

injection into their economy of White skill, capital and enterprise.

(5) All this should make it possible for South Africans to set themselves, as an ultimate ideal, a racial federation in South Africa.

It became clear, too, that many of the 'intellectuals' among the Afrikaners disagreed with Verwoerd's policy. Two prominent Dutch Reformed Church theologians, Professor A. S. Geyser and Professor A. van Selms, circulated a memorandum in which they condemned Apartheid as selfish and an offence against human dignity. They declared that measures like the Group Areas Act, job reservation, the pass laws and the Separate Representation of Voters Act encroached upon human dignity, justice, freedom and peace. 'We submit,' they said, 'that Apartheid is, and will be, of necessity a total failure. All the hardships, injustices and injuries it inflicts in the meantime have been of no effect except to aggravate the legacy of suspicion and hatred for future generations.'

After South Africa decided to leave the Commonwealth it was bitterly attacked at the meetings of the United Nations. It was noted that Britain and France who formerly always abstained from voting on anti-South African resolutions now voted for many of them.

In the United Nations Special Political Committee in April 1961 Ghana proposed that all members should ban trade with South Africa and deny the use of their ports and aerodromes to South African ships and planes. The motion was carried by 41 votes to 32, but did not secure the two-thirds majority required to obtain endorsement of the proposal by the Assembly. A milder resolution recommending 'separate and collective action' by member States to end South Africa's discriminatory laws was carried by ninety-three votes to one.

The Special Political Committee also voted in favour of 'exploring the continued disregard' by South Africa of Assembly resolutions on Apartheid and its 'application of further discriminatory laws and measures, the enforcement of which had led to violence and bloodshed'.

The General Assembly continued to ask that South-West Africa should be placed under a trusteeship agreement. It held that South Africa had no right to control the territory, and that the Natives in it were not being treated in accordance with the terms of the mandate granted after the First World War. The question of the future of the ex-German colony seems likely to lead to a prolonged dispute between the United Nations and the South African Government in the near future.

Critics of the Apartheid policy chided the Government with making only a half-hearted effort to establish its Bantustans. In February 1961 the Minister of Bantu Administration announced that a five year plan had been drawn up for the development of the eight population units, and it would now proceed 'at an increased tempo and in an energetic manner.' The scheme comprised three main points:

(1) Reclamation, rehabilitation and development of the soil and natural resources of the Bantu areas.
(2) The purchase of land at a faster tempo than in the past in the execution of the Native Trust and Land Act of 1936.
(3) What may be called human development.

To implement the plan a Director of Bantu Development was appointed and was specially charged with the task of securing 'the accelerated development of the Bantu as a person and of the Bantu areas'.

In view of the increasingly hostile attitude of many overseas countries the Opposition appealed to the Government to make concessions in its colour policy. Verwoerd insisted, however, that only by separate development could the future of the Whites be assured. Even the Coloureds might in time have an independent state within the republic which, like the Bantustans, would work in harmony with the White state. The Johannesburg *Star* remarked that Afrikaner Nationalism was 'embarking on another Great Trek—this time a great trek of the mind away from the world into a Never Never Land with no geographical reality.'

The idea of setting up well-defined Non-White states without further delay appealed to many Afrikaners. They felt that such a step would prove the genuineness of the separate development policy and would placate world opinion, which was running more and more strongly against them. They argued that if the people abroad saw that the different races in South Africa were actually being established in their own territories most of the condemnation to which the Nationalist Government had been subjected would fall away. Positive action would show that the Apartheid plan was not merely a smoke screen to conceal the continuance of White domination but a practical policy by which all the Non-Whites would be able to work out their own future in their own way.

When the Territorial Authority in the Transkei met in April 1961 some of the members asked the Government to draft a constitution giving the territory independence. The Minister for Bantu Affairs said that independence might be granted 'in a few years'. It all depended on the Bantu themselves and their ability to take over the administration. But he added: 'In the towns of the Transkei, as long as there are Whites—which of course will be for many generations—the Whites will be directly governed by the White Government. The Bantu will rule only their own people.'

In the White areas the 'Black spots' are being removed. In the Black areas the 'White spots' are apparently to remain indefinitely.

The Government had from time to time assured the public that the men banished to detention camps lived under easy and comfortable conditions. In April 1961 the Institute of Race Relations published a report on the state in which its investigator had found sixty-two Natives who had been banished by the Government without trial. They were, it said, living 'in remote and desolate areas' and subjected to the extremes of 'poverty and humiliation'. 'Men who are chiefs, teachers, students or trade unionists,' declared the report, 'are given work as labourers or put to herding cattle, or if there is no work they are left to pass the years in idleness.' When they were given work they received £5 a month from which they paid for their food, clothing, bedding and furniture and supported their families. Those who were not given work were entitled to an allowance of £2 a month, but not all the unemployed received it. 'The conditions under which the deportees and their families are obliged to live,' said the report, 'are greatly at variance with the Minister's assurances about their treatment.'

On May 31, 1961, the Republic of South Africa was formally proclaimed at Pretoria with a big military display and much rejoicing among the Afrikaners. The majority of the English held aloof. The Non-Whites organized demonstrations against the change in the constitution.

Verwoerd once more assured the public that under the republic South Africa would be a happy country with a bright and prosperous future.

This spirit of confidence was far from universal.

The Republic still faced the racial problem that had plagued the Union under the monarchy. The façade had been painted a different colour. The insecure racial structure behind it had not been altered.

CHAPTER XI

Can Apartheid Succeed?

Nowhere in the world is there a more difficult—and more dangerous—problem of colour and race than that which faces the Republic of South Africa.

In the not distant future the greater part of the continent south of the Sahara will be ruled by Africans. Even in the British White settler areas the Europeans realize that the Natives must be given an increasing share in the administration, and the necessary changes will doubtless be made without serious strife.

In the Republic of South Africa, however, there are three million Whites, the majority of whom are inflexible in their determination not to share authority with the twelve million Non-Whites among whom they live. They vow that they would rather perish than allow their homeland to be governed by another race. Only a very small minority favour the building up of a multi-racial society in which there would be no discrimination on the ground of colour alone. But so strong is the feeling of the mass of the Whites that even the official Opposition in Parliament—the United Party—in the unlikely event of being returned to power, would not be able to offer concessions acceptable to the Non-Europeans.

The obstacle to a peaceful solution of the colour question is the deep-rooted sentiment of the people once called the South African Dutch, but now known as the Afrikaners, who form the majority of the Whites in the republic.

Distant observers do not realize the intensity of the spirit in which the Afrikaners approach the problem of the future of their homeland. On it they will not compromise. They are Calvinists who are convinced that God established them at the foot of Africa and led them through many dangers, and they are prepared to die in defence of their heritage.

Such is their temper that it has been said that if the Afrikaners
had to choose between their religion and their policy of colour
discrimination they would jettison their religion.

In a leading article in April 1961 the *Transvaler* (the National
Party newspaper that Verwoerd once edited) said that the Afrikaner
'believes that his ideal of continued existence for the White man
in South Africa will be crowned with success. The Afrikaner
believes in the paramountcy of God. He believes that he was
brought to South Africa by the Supreme Being with a divine
purpose, and the realization of that purpose is for him the primary
task and a matter of principle about which there can be no
speculation to seek material well-being and temporary advantage.'

'When a divine calling has to be fulfilled,' declared the paper,
'self-interest and opportunism do not count.' It went on to recall
Afrikaner history and enumerate the sacrifices that Afrikaner men,
women and children had made in the past for the sake of their
ideals. 'What counted with all of them,' it said, 'was that the
ideals and principles would continue to exist, for this guidance
is exalted high above the sphere of speculative argument even
though a Higher Hand should determine that he who fights for
the principle has to go under in the struggle.'

In his book, *Inside the South African Crucible*, Professor Dr.
A. B. Dupreez, a prominent theologian of the Dutch Reformed
Church, insisted that White and Black must live apart. 'South
Africa's one and only hope,' he wrote, 'lies in the application of
autogeneous development for national service which enables the
different racial groups to live their own lives in a becoming way,
to realize their human dignity, and to be free. Only by following
this road will we be obeying our Divine vocation. And if we
nevertheless disappear from the southern corner of Africa and
perish as a White nation, then we declare in good conscience
before the whole world and in the name of the Afrikaner people
that we prefer (as King David after God's judgment was
announced) not to die by our own hand on the fatal road of
integration and assimilation but rather at the hand of God himself
who controls our destinies. If the Non-Whites should cruelly
murder us and cut us to pieces it would indeed be a new triumph
of the barbarism God so wonderfully halted at Blood River.
Nevertheless, we firmly believe, as a matter of faith, that God still
mercifully rules the destinies of our nation. Rather than fuse with

the Non-Whites and lose our identity and Divine vocation we prefer to perish on the road of obedience, as God has taught us.'

It is upon this plane that Verwoerd views the vital problems that confront his country. He is a dedicated man and surrounds himself with dedicated men. They are convinced that separation on the ground of the colour of the skin is right and just and has scriptural sanction. Upon that issue he will never negotiate. He will enforce his policy relentlessly no matter what the ultimate outcome may be.

With very few exceptions the Afrikaners are of the same mind —and a considerable number of the English section stand with him. Thus there is very little prospect of the Afrikaners being defeated at the polls when they appeal to the country on the cry that the White race is in danger.

The world of 1961 rejects the idea that the problem of race and colour in South Africa can be solved by the establishment of White and Black states. Yet sixty years ago the plan was suggested by many responsible people, and under favourable conditions it might have been adopted with general approval. Had it been implemented with large scale immigration and the inclusion of the High Commission Territories in South Africa, the separate development scheme might have been practicable. The influx of Natives into the White areas had not swelled to the flood that followed the rapid industrialization of recent times. The Natives were then content to do the rough work of the country and did not aspire to take the White man's place.

The inclusion in South Africa of the High Commission Territories—usually known as the Protectorates—would have given a fairly equitable distribution of the land between the Whites and the Blacks. With it there would be 357,421 square miles of territory reserved for the Blacks, and 408,494 for the Whites. Instead of having only the eleven per cent of the country reserved for them today the Blacks would hold forty-two per cent.

Indeed when the Union of South Africa was formed it was expected that the Protectorates would soon be incorporated in it. Article 151 of the South Africa Act made specific provision for the transfer, although no date was fixed. Had the National Convention agreed to extend the Cape franchise (which had no colour bar) to the whole of the Union, the transfer might have been made in 1910. But the constitution drafted by the Convention left the franchise to be decided by the Union Parliament and laid down that only Whites could sit in its legislature. The British Government then held that the aboriginal population in the Protectorates would have to be consulted before they were transferred, and also that the British Parliament would have to discuss the matter.

From time to time the Union asked for the transfer, and in 1952 Dr. Malan threatened that if nothing were done the Union might regard the Protectorates as 'foreign territory'. In 1954 the Union Parliament adopted a resolution declaring that it 'resolved' that the transfer 'should take place as soon as possible' and that negotiations with Britain should be resumed. There were further talks but agreement was never reached.

The Afrikaners still hold that they have a right to the territories —or at least to the two smaller ones—for geographically they form part of South Africa and are closely linked with it economically. They cherish the hope that one day the transfer may yet be made and thus give a more reasonable look to their policy of separate development.

The three High Commission Territories are:

(i) Basutoland, with an area of 11,716 square miles and a population of approximately 750,000. It became involved in a war with the Orange Free State Boers and in 1866 the ruling chief Moshesh acknowledged himself a subject of the Free State. The war broke out again and the country was placed under British protection and was for a time annexed to the Cape Colony. Had it not been for the intervention of Great Britain the country might, the Afrikaners argue, have formed part of the Free State and so today be included in the Republic of South Africa.

(2) Bechuanaland, covering 275,000 square miles with a population of 360,000. The Boers from the Transvaal infiltrated into the area and clashed with the Natives and a British protectorate was proclaimed which prevented the Boers occupying the territory.

(3) Swaziland, with an area of 6,705 square miles and a population of about 230,000. From 1894 onwards the country was actually administered by the Transvaal, although it was not incorporated in Kruger's republic. This form of control lasted until the Anglo-Boer war of 1899-1902 when the territory was placed under the Lieutenant-Governor of the Transvaal. In 1906 the Transvaal received responsible government, and Swaziland was handed over to the High Commission.

The Tomlinson Commission calculated that South Africa was responsible for providing the means of existence for nearly half the population of Basutoland, one-third of the population of Swaziland, and one-fifth of the population of Bechuanaland.

Despite the withdrawal of South Africa from the Commonwealth the question of the Protectorates may be raised again. The Afrikaners hold that the existence of the three territories under the control of an outside government, but within the geographical framework of South Africa, is an anomaly no less than would be the existence of Scotland or Wales as a French protectorate governed from France although enjoying all the benefits of close financial relations with England. Their economy is based mainly upon their trade with South Africa and the employment within it of a large number of their inhabitants who send money back to their homes.

In 1954 a leading British churchman—the Rev. L. B. Greaves, secretary of the British Council of Churches—paid a lengthy visit to South and Central Africa. He reported that various statements had led him to expect that ninety per cent of the Basutos were opposed to incorporation in South Africa. When he visited the country however he found a considerable volume of opinion in favour of incorporation. He wrote: 'Natives said that they would gain by incorporation better pay, more assured food supplies, more efficient schools and health services.'

Verwoerd has not abandoned all hope of associating the Protectorates with South Africa in some way. Speaking in Parliament on March 24, 1961, he said:

> 'I disagree with the British Government's policy for the Protectorates. I do not think it does justice to the Black man. Basutoland for instance is a Black man's country and should be developed as such. But Britain is developing a multi-racial state. If Basutoland fell under the protection of the Union Government we would not allow the two thousand White people there to have the vote. We would lead it in the direction of development as a Black man's country.'

The Afrikaners feel that the Protectorates may become a potential danger to their country. If developed under British policy they might fall into hands hostile to the Whites in South Africa. They point to the fact that people charged with defying South African laws have escaped to Basutoland and been accepted as political refugees. They fear that the Protectorates may become the headquarters of organizations planning subversive movements in the republic.

An influential Afrikaans paper, *Dagbreek*, suggests that Britain and South Africa should enter into a joint guardianship over the three territories as a preliminary to their ultimate incorporation in the republic on the lines of the Bantu areas. Basutoland presents a particularly difficult problem because it is entirely surrounded by South African territory. The relationship between the republic and the British colonial territories may give rise to some troublesome issues in the future.

Whatever may be the ultimate fate of the Protectorates it is clear that for the present the policy of separate development in South Africa will have to be applied to a territory in which the Blacks who form four-fifths of the population have reserved for them only between one-eighth and one-ninth of the land. The Native Reserves set aside under the 1913 Land Act covered 22.7 million acres, though additional land could be purchased in the 'released areas'. Through the Trust Fund set aside in 1936 the Government has spent £12m. in buying more land, but there are some five million acres in the 'released areas' still to be added to the Reserves. If this additional ground is secured the Bantu areas will comprise 41.8 million acres, or 64,348 square miles out of the republic's 472,685 square miles. The Government claims that the Bantu areas will be twice the size of England and Wales, four times that of Denmark, five-and-a-half times that of Belgium and so on. Some of the 'intellectuals' among the Afrikaners admit that the land reserved for the Bantu is far too small. They suggest that the Reserves should be made into viable economic blocks even if some of the White towns have to be included in them. They declare that half the surface of the country ought to be reserved for the Bantu to make the Apartheid plan a permanent solution of the problem. It is unlikely that the White electorate could be induced to sanction so drastic a measure.

The basis of the Apartheid plan is the development of the Bantu homelands agriculturally and industrially so that they can carry a much larger population and reduce the number of the Bantu in the White areas to manageable proportions.

Today these areas are badly farmed, over-stocked and much eroded. In them the Bantu are eventually to enjoy political independence in friendly association with White South Africa. But the majority of the Afrikaners assert that it will take two hundred years to make the Bantu sufficiently advanced to receive full self-government.

Whatever the future of South Africa may be, it is obviously desirable that the Bantu areas should be rescued from their present backward condition. No sensible person objects to the vigorous development plan upon which the Government has embarked. A comprehensive programme of betterment is being carried out—indeed some Afrikaners feel that too much is being spent on the Natives and not enough on the poorer Whites.

In the Bantu areas between 1948 and 1957 more than £12m. have been expended on agriculture and afforestation. The Natives are being taught modern farming methods and, to guide the campaign of instruction, a staff of three hundred and fifty European officers are employed, and approximately the same number of fully trained Bantu assistants. In time all the Europeans will be replaced by Bantu. Thousands of miles of fencing have been put up, two hundred conservation dams constructed, and twenty-two breeding stations provided for the improvement of the herds owned by the Natives. Sugar and fibre are being grown, and saw-mills have been provided as the beginning of a timber industry. The Bantu Investment Corporation has been launched with a capital of £500,000 to help the Natives to start industrial and commercial enterprises.

Five or six Bantu capitals are to be built. In each capital there will be stationed a Commissioner-General who will represent the Prime Minister and be the adviser of the Bantu. It is also intended to set up Bantu consulates in White cities where there are many Natives. Since 1954 twenty-five towns have been laid out in the Bantu areas, and a further thirty-eight are in various stages of development. Farming land is to be worked only by full-time Bantu farmers, and the non-farming section of the community will be offered other means of making a living through industrial, commercial, professional or administrative employment in the new towns.

The Government, however, do not propose to make the Bantu areas a national home for a Bantu nation. They are to be the homelands of eight different tribes, so that there will be a Zulu block, a Xosas block, a Swazi block and so on, each with their own language and way of life.

The Tomlinson Commission found that the Bantu areas comprised 110 units, and in addition there were 154 'Black spots', and it recommended that many of the smaller areas should be merged into larger ones to create economic units. So far this has not been done; and the leaders of the African National Congress assert that the Government's policy is really designed to keep the Bantu divided and weak. The Bantustans, too, are being created upon a tribal basis. The Government appoints the chiefs and headmen, controls all activities, and supervises education from the primary schools to the university.

The economic development of the Bantu areas is certainly all to the good. It will raise the standard of living of the inhabitants and provide new spheres of activity for the more enterprising among them.

What is.not so certain is whether the Natives in them will be content to live indefinitely under a tribal system. Nor is it certain that the Bantu in the White areas, who are to have their homelands in the Reserves, will find the way of life there acceptable. Tribalism cannot last in the modern world even though under-pinned by governments. The Bantu both in the Reserves and in the White areas are becoming westernized, and they may resent White control, for many years to come, of the only area in which they have any chance of developing to the full extent of their capacity. Indeed in the changing climate of opinion all over Africa the chiefs and headmen in the Reserves may themselves be moved by the spirit of African nationalism emerging among their own people. In the not very distant future the Bantustans may house a population revealing a temper that may make their relations with White South Africa increasingly difficult.

In any case, only about one-third of the Bantu live in the Reserves. Another third are employed by European landowners under a variety of conditions. The rest are scattered over the White areas, and in all the towns they outnumber the Whites. Johannesburg, for example, has 389,690 Whites and about 650,000 Blacks. Verwoerd and his colleagues admit that the present distribution of the Bantu is an obstacle to the application of the separate development policy. They insist however that with the advance of the Bantu areas the position will change. They say that in twenty years' time the Reserves will offer so many opportunities that the Bantu in the towns will flow back to them. The Whites are to do more of the work in their own areas, while the Blacks will migrate to the Bantustans in which they will find no colour ceiling over their head. White immigration—which the

Afrikaners opposed for many years—is now to be encouraged with that end in view.

At present no such movement is perceptible. Indeed the Nationalist Government has made the towns much more attractive to the Blacks. Slums have been swept away on a gigantic scale. Between 1950 and 1959 it advanced funds to the local authorities which enabled 133,617 full-sized two-, three- and four-roomed houses to be built providing accommodation for over half a million people, while hostels were erected for unmarried men. Sport stadiums, recreation halls and other amenities were provided, and the Bantu had a monopoly of the trading stores in the townships. The urban Natives in South Africa are on the whole better fed, dressed and housed than those in any other African territory.

But they are fast becoming a westernized people among whom there is growing discontent at the conditions under which they are compelled to live. Among many of them there seems to be a feeling of cynical despair, though beneath the surface there burns a bitter resentment that may before long be blown into a flame. They feel they are humiliated and frustrated at every turn, and regarded as an inferior race who can never be more than drudges for their White overlords, some of whom look upon them with open disdain. There are still Whites in South Africa who forget the old saying: 'Many can bear adversity, few can bear contempt.'

The Bantu look with suspicion on the education provided for them by the Government. They think that instruction through their mother tongue is part of a plan to maintain separate tribes and encourage them to cherish old antagonisms. In former days in the mission schools the teaching was in English, and they prefer it even if it means the gradual disappearance of the Bantu languages. They want to learn English because it is a *lingua franca* for all Bantu and gives them command of a tongue in which they can obtain the books essential for advanced education. They see in the Apartheid policy in the Reserves and the White areas alike a subtle scheme for keeping them a backward people.

The crux of the racial problem in South Africa clearly lies in the White areas, and particularly in the White industrial areas. There a large Non-White proletariat is growing up. It is composed of town-bred or town-born people who have no ties with the Reserves and no desire to remove to them. Barred by law from all but the roughest and lowest paid tasks, and harassed by inumerable restrictions and discriminations, they are perpetually irritated by the conditions under which they live. Will the assurance that if if they move to some distant Bantustan they will be free from colour bars make them content with their inferior position ? Is it not certain that, watching the advance of their fellows in other parts of Africa, they will demand the right to enjoy freedom and a voice in the administration of the area in which they live and work ? If all concessions are denied them will they not launch movements designed to force the Whites to ease their lot ? And in that event will they not be able to rely upon the sympathy, and perhaps the active support, of their compatriots in the Bantustans ?

Thus events in the next few years will depend upon the temper of the Blacks in the White areas. It is they who will decide whether there is to be peace or unrest. They are more westernized than their fellows in the Bantu homelands. They are more inclined to be moved by the spirit of Black nationalism—which cannot be halted at the borders of the republic no matter what repressive measures are taken against those who preach it. They know that whatever form their protests may take they will have the backing of every independent African State and of many oversea peoples. Will they be satisfied with promises of 'pie in the sky' in the shape of full freedom in some far-off Bantustan ?

Moreover, the Black population in the White areas is increasing faster than the White. The Tomlinson Commission estimated that if present trends continue there will at the end of the century be fifteen million Bantu in the urban areas outside the Bantu areas. 'Unless,' declared the Commission, 'economic development can be diverted from its present geographical concentration, no other result can be expected than that the relative share of the Bantu in the composition of the urban areas will increase.'

Verwoerd claims that this can be done by setting up industries on the borders of the Reserves so that large numbers of the Bantu will leave the towns to live in the Bantu areas and work in the across-the-border factories. He calculates that with the vigorous application of his policy there will in the year 2000 be only six million Bantu in the White areas. Where the other fifteen million Bantu, who will be in the country by that time, are to live and work has not been made clear. Presumably they are to crowd into the Reserves.

But at present there is not the faintest indication that so drastic a change in the distribution of the population can be achieved.

The economy of South Africa is based upon the use of Non-European labour for all unskilled and semi-skilled work. There is not the slightest sign in agriculture, or industry or any other activity, that employers are prepared to use White labour on a large scale. So as industrial expansion continues more and more Blacks will work in the White areas. More houses are being built for them in the Native townships, and it is not suggested that these vast settlements are to become 'ghost towns' in the near future.

All the Blacks in the White areas are to be regarded as foreigners. They are to be classed as migrant labourers who when their working life is over will retire to their homelands in the Bantu areas. They will not be treated as permanent citizens of White South Africa, for they will have their own homelands in which they will enjoy political rights. Thus, argue the Nationalists, there will be no political rivalry between White and Black. The Blacks will have no claim to be represented in Parliament for they will have their own legislative bodies in their own territories.

The majority of the Whites do not anticipate a drastic reduction in the number of Non-Whites in the White areas. But they do not view the situation with anxiety. They believe that with higher wages, and better housing and more amenities, the Bantu in the urban centres will be content to do the unskilled work for the Whites. They boast that their Natives have a higher standard of living than those in the new African States and say that the bulk of them will be so comfortably off that they will accept their restricted way of life during their working years and will eventually retire to the Reserves.

History does not encourage the complacent expectation that with an improvement in their economic condition the Bantu in the towns will always accept the inferior position to which they are condemned. It is true that today many of them are so concerned in earning a living that they pay little attention to politics. The African National Congress has never had the number of active members that one might have expected from the size of the population to which it appeals. Indeed the Government claims that ninety-nine per cent of the Bantu are well-disposed towards the separate development idea and realize that they will gain more under it than they would by being inferior citizens in a multi-racial state. But for 'agitators and instigators', say the supporters of Apartheid, the mass of the Blacks would gladly accept the Government's plans for their future.

The story of the advance of the human race does not support these optimistic ideas. It does not sanction the hypothesis that a little more comfort will make men content with an inferior place in society. Discontent really gains force when conditions improve. De Tocqueville noted in his studies of the French revolution that the French masses found their position the more intolerable the better it became.

The historian Arnold Toynbee has pointed out that racial conflicts are more likely to come to a crisis where a civilized minority lives with its progeny side by side with an under-privileged majority. The minority must either accept, relying on their own merits, an unprivileged position among the less cultured majority, or else try to hold on to their domination by force. But the threat and use of force in social administration has ever proved to be an Achilles' heel.

Viewed through rose-hued spectacles the plan of separate development may present a pleasing appearance to those who want to find an easy way of escape from an extremely difficult situation.

But the hard fact is that in South Africa today a White aristocracy, or privileged class, numbering three millions, decides the way of life for many more millions of under-privileged people, the bulk of whom can never be more than the hewers of wood and drawers of water for their rulers. Their only hope of being able to rise to the full extent of their capacity lies in migrating to a distant area which can never contain more than a percentage of them.

The under-privileged majority complain bitterly of the pass laws, the police raids and the rebuffs and frustrations to which they are subjected by the system of colour discrimination imposed by the White majority. They follow with keen interest the changes being made in other parts of Africa. They hear the leaders of the independent African States declare that they will do their utmost to win freedom for Africans in every territory in the continent. They resent the stamp of inferiority more strongly than their fathers did.

The African in the towns will not submit as quietly as once he did to the insults, and often the blows, showered upon him by a good many Whites despite the efforts of the Government to stamp out such abuses. Europeans who know the townships and the locations say that there is far more bitter feeling against the Whites than there was a generation ago. Will these people submit quietly to conditions that they know are condemned by most of the rest of the world? How widespread is this condemnation was admitted by the Afrikaans *Die Burger* which declared bitterly that South Africa had become 'the polecat of the nations'.

If the Blacks in the White areas defy the laws under which they live they can of course be held down by force. There are many South Africans who believe that the colour problem can be solved by guns and tear gas, and that the sooner they are used the better.

The possibility of an armed conflict cannot be entirely ruled out; yet a cold war is more likely than a shooting one. The leaders of the Non-Whites realize that in such a struggle they would be at a great disadvantage. They insist that they are opposed to violence and will fight with the only weapons they possess—boycotts, strikes and passive resistance.

Non-violent campaigns may end in clashes with the police, especially if militant groups thrust their way to the front. Today, however, the African National Congress and its associated bodies protest that they have no intention of taking up arms; and unless the whole situation changes for the worse they will probably continue to press their claims by passive methods. In their efforts they will have the support of all the Non-White peoples who resent colour discrimination as an insult to their own race. There are twenty-four independent African States who are likely to boycott South Africa in various ways, and some of the Asian nations may follow suit.

Such in broad outline are the conditions under which the policy of Apartheid and the rival policy of building up a multi-racial society are being presented to the South African electorate. Today the separate development party returns the government, and for a long time to come the cry that the White race is in danger will be sufficient to ensure its victory at the polls. The more loudly the Non-Whites demand equality the stronger grows the fear of the Whites that their future is threatened and the more determined they are to maintain in power the party pledged to enforce colour separation.

The Nationalists are unshakably convinced that their policy is right and just, and they will continue to implement it no matter what hardships or sacrifices have to be faced.

If the majority of the Whites go forward in this spirit the colour issue must lead to a long and bitter struggle. Whatever the Nationalist leaders may say, there is no prospect of greatly reducing the preponderance of the Blacks in the White areas. The bulk of these who shout for Apartheid will not do without the Black labour upon which the industries of the country are based —any serious attempt to do so would result in so disastrous an upheaval in the national economy that it is doubtful whether even the Afrikaners could be persuaded to vote for it. Job reservation enforced on the gigantic scale necessary to reduce the number of Blacks in the White areas to a minority would have the same effect. Applied as it is today it is only an additional irritant to the Non-Whites.

The Nationalist Government in the republic, as under the monarchy, will continue to decide the way of life of an ever-increasing Non-White majority in the urban areas and will ruthlessly suppress any movement that threatens their supremacy.

But the Non-Whites are becoming a westernized people: and number is their strength. The more they rise in the scale of civilization the more strongly will they resent a system under which they will be an unprivileged class ruled by a relatively small minority of another race. All history is a warning against the dangers inherent in such a situation.

When nearly all Africa is governed by Africans, can the Whites at the foot of the continent rule indefinitely a Non-White population outnumbering them by four or five to one?

Long ago, even among the Afrikaners, there were those who rejected the soothing belief that the Natives in Africa would accept permanent domination by the White man. When in 1909 the National Convention sat to draft a constitution for the union of the four British colonies there was a dispute over the site for the capital of the united country. 'Onze' Jan Hofmeyr, the head of the Afrikaner Bond, favoured Cape Town. He wrote:

'If the capital goes to Pretoria then it will not return before the gold mines are exhausted or the great Native upheaval of the interior is in full swing. Cape Town will appear to be the last stronghold of the European settlements in South Africa.'

Fifty years later it is clear that the gold mines are far from being exhausted and are likely to last for many years. But it is obvious that 'the great Native upheaval of the interior' is in full swing and that it must have serious repercussions at the foot of the continent.

The Afrikaners are not to be moved by warnings or threats. They are unshaken in their faith that a Higher Hand has placed them in South Africa, and that it is their duty to hold it for their children and their children's children. They are forming their laager for a last stand against the hordes of barbarism: and if Providence ordains that they must go down they will go down fighting.

The tragedy of the situation is that a complete deadlock has been reached, and that there seems to be no way of breaking it. Whites and Non-Whites alike are convinced that the stand they are taking today is justified by their past. Both insist that they are fighting for freedom and the right to achieve the future that Providence designed for them.

If the Whites would lay the foundations of a multi-racial society—in which they would, by reason of their greater advancement, be the dominant force for many years—the problem of the future relationship of Black and White might be solved without a violent conflict. The changes made would be evolutionary and not revolutionary. The Whites would have time to adjust themselves to an environment which, though new to them, would be found over the rest of the world.

Together White and Non-White could build a great country at the foot of Africa. Locked in a struggle for supremacy both must suffer, no matter which side ultimately emerges victorious.

Yet there is no hope of agreement. The colour war in South Africa has begun. It must rage for a long time before even an armistice is possible.

The basic issue may be temporarily obscured by an attempt to divide the country into White and Black States—an experiment that might create new and unforeseen complications in the political and economic field.

But the root question will remain: Can a White minority in the modern world dominate indefinitely a large Non-White majority?

Only wishful-thinking can answer it in the affirmative.

POSTSCRIPT

The Republic of South Africa was proclaimed on May 31, 1961, under conditions tantamount to a state of emergency.

An All-In African Conference had been held at Maritzburg at which a resolution was passed calling on the Government to summon a national convention to draft a constitution for a multi-racial State. This was sent to Verwoerd with a threat that if nothing were done there would be a stay-at-home strike and country-wide demonstrations on May 29, 30 and 31. Verwoerd described the letter as 'arrogant' and did not answer it.

The Government then received reports that certain organizations planned to interrupt the inaugural ceremony on May 31. To avoid having to proclaim a state of emergency the Government took drastic action to prevent any anti-republican activities on that day. On May 19 all meetings and gatherings were banned until June 26 under a penalty of a fine of £200. The ban was so widely drawn that permits had to be obtained for weddings, concerts, sports meetings and indeed any assembly of even two or three people. In Johannesburg five thousand permits were applied for, and in Cape Town nearly four thousand, in order to maintain the ordinary everyday life of the community.

The Government also rushed through Parliament an Act which enabled the Attorney-General to refuse bail to arrested persons for a period of twelve days, thus confining them to prison for that period without being brought to court and formally charged. Under this new law thousands of people (mainly Non-Whites) were arrested and jailed. Then the most extensive military alert ever known in South Africa in peace time was ordered. Five thousand men of the Active Citizen Force and the burgher commandos were called up and placed in camps in what were regarded as potentially troublesome areas; and military guards were mounted to protect public works and buildings.

Verwoerd said that these steps had been taken to ensure that the republic was born 'in an atmosphere of reverence'.

The stay-at-home strike was fifty per cent effective in some areas on May 29, but collapsed on the following day. The inauguration of the Republic on May 31 at Pretoria passed off without incident; and on June 6 the ban on meetings was lifted.

At the end of June the police began to set up road blocks all over the country and arrested thousands of 'loafers', passless Natives and criminals. These 'swoops' lasted for several months and resulted, it was claimed, in a marked decrease of crime.

Police were placed on the frontiers of the republic and of South West Africa to prevent the infiltration of Natives from neighbouring territories. The number of men called up for training in the Active Citizen Force was doubled: and the Minister of Defence stated that the Government aimed at having a force of sixty thousand trained men always available for any emergency. Women were encouraged to learn to shoot, and revolver clubs were formed for them in which instruction was given by police officers. The latest tanks and quick-firing rifles were ordered from Europe for the army.

The Government announced that it would speed up the development of the Bantu homelands. The Bantu in the White areas would be able to elect their own town councils; but they would never be given a say in the administration of the White areas, in which they would always be regarded as migrant labourers even though they might have been born in them. Verwoerd declared that he would 'stand like granite' on the separate development policy, which was the only one that could solve the race problems of the Republic. For the first time he appointed a Minister of Coloured Affairs and a Minister of Indian Affairs, and said that the two groups would eventually manage their own affairs in their own areas with a Parliament on a 'State within a State' basis; but they would not be given the independence which the Bantu homelands might ultimately enjoy.

Although the legislature of the Republic could run to 1963, Verwoerd announced that there would be a general election on October 18, 1961. As the Nationalist Government is certain of being returned again the appeal to the country will give Verwoerd five years of practically unchallenged power in which to prove that his four-stream vertical separate development theory can be made into a workable policy for solving the race problem in the Republic of South Africa.

Johannesburg,

  September, 1961.

SOME BOOKS CONSULTED

AGAR-HAMILTON, J. A. I.: *The Native Policy of the Voortrekkers.*
BOURQUIN, REV. C.: *The Union's Native Problem.*
BROOKES, E. H.: *The Colour Problems of South Africa.*
BUXTON, EARL: *General Botha.*
DE KIEWIET, C. W.: *A History of South Africa.*
DUPREEZ, Professor A. B.: *Inside the South African Crucible.*
EVANS, IFOR L.: *Native Policy in Southern Africa.*
EVANS, MAURICE: *Black and White in South East Africa.*
FITZPATRICK, SIR PERCY: *The Transvaal from Within.*
HEADLAM, CECIL: *The Milner Papers.*
HOERNLE, R. F. A.: *South African Native Policy and the Liberal Spirit.*
  „ „ „ : *Race and Reason.*
HOFMEYR, J. H.: *The Life of Jan Hendrik Hofmeyr.*
HUDDLESTON, TREVOR: *Naught for Your Comfort.*
KEET, B. B.: *Whither South Africa?*
KUPER, LEO: *Passive Resistance in SOUTH Africa.*
LEVI, N.: *Jan Smuts*
LONG, B. K.: *In Smut's Camp.*
MACMILLAN, W. M.: *The Cape Colour Problem.*
  „ „ „ : *Bantu, Boer and Briton.*
McDONALD, J. G.: *Rhodes: A Life.*
MARAIS, J. S.: *The Cape Coloured People.*
MAY, HENRY JOHN: *The South African Constitution.*
MICHELL, SIR LEWIS: *The Life of the Rt. Hon. Cecil John Rhodes.*
NATHAN, MANFRED: *Paul Kruger.*
NIELSON, PETER: *The Colour Bar.*
PATTERSON, SHEILA: *The Last Trek.*
REITZ, DR. HJALMAR: *The Conversion of a South African Nationalist.*
ROUX, EDWARD: *Time Longer then Rope.*
SAMPSON, ANTHONY: *Treason Cage.*
  „ „ : *Drum.*
STEWARD, A. W.: *You Are Wrong Father Huddleston.*
THEAL, G. M.: *History of South Africa since 1795.*
TOEKOMS, JAN: *South Africa's Eleventh Hour.*
  „ „ : *When Malan Goes.*
VAN DEN HEEVER, C. M.: *General J. M. B. Hertzog.*
VAN DER HORST, SHEILA T.: *Native Labour in South Africa.*
WALKER, ERIC A.: *A History of South Africa.*
WETHERELL, VIOLET: *The Indian Question in South Africa.*

See also *A Survey of Race Relations in South Africa* issued annually
by the South African Institute of Race Relations; the *Hansard of the
Union Parliament* from 1910 to 1960; the reports of South African
Commissions on Native Affairs.